To Stephenie Meyer, David Slade, and the entire cast and crew
who brought the world of ECLIPSE to life;
And to Edris Dade, who shared all those TWILIGHT moments in the dark . . .
—M.C.V.

A major feature film can be made up of hundreds of talented artists representing
various crafts and disciplines. *The Twilight Saga: Eclipse* is no exception.
The following gave insights into the broad strokes of making this film, and we
thank them for the generosity of their time and their enthusiasm for the work:

ROB FRIEDMAN, CO-CHAIRMAN AND CEO, SUMMIT ENTERTAINMENT

PATRICK WACHSBERGER, CO-CHAIRMAN AND PRESIDENT, SUMMIT ENTERTAINMENT

DAVID SLADE, DIRECTOR

MELISSA ROSENBERG, SCREENWRITER

WYCK GODFREY, PRODUCER

KAREN ROSENFELT, PRODUCER

BILL BANNERMAN, CO-PRODUCER

JAVIER AGUIRRESAROBE, DIRECTOR OF PHOTOGRAPHY

PAUL DENHAM AUSTERBERRY, PRODUCTION DESIGNER

TISH MONAGHAN, COSTUME DESIGNER

JEREMY BALL, PRODUCTION VISUAL EFFECTS COORDINATOR

PHIL TIPPETT, VISUAL EFFECTS SUPERVISOR, TIPPETT STUDIO

TOM GIBBONS, ANIMATION SUPERVISOR, TIPPETT STUDIO

ERIC LEVEN, VISUAL EFFECTS SUPERVISOR, TIPPETT STUDIO

JON COWLEY, VISUAL EFFECTS SUPERVISOR, IMAGE ENGINE

ROBIN HACKL, SEQUENCE SUPERVISOR AND ON-SET PLATE SUPERVISOR,
IMAGE ENGINE

SHAWN WALSH, VISUAL EFFECTS EXECUTIVE PRODUCER, IMAGE ENGINE

CHARLES PORLIER, MAKEUP DESIGNER

JOANN FOWLER, MAKEUP HEAD, SECOND UNIT

GINA SHERRITT, KEY HAIRSTYLIST

ALEX BURDETT, SPECIAL EFFECTS SUPERVISOR

JOHN STONEHAM JR., STUNT COORDINATOR

JONATHAN EUSEBIO, FIGHT COORDINATOR

KIMBERLEY FRENCH, SET PHOTOGRAPHER

DOANE GREGORY, PHOTOGRAPHER, SECOND UNIT

ERIK FEIG, PRESIDENT OF PRODUCTION & ACQUISITIONS, SUMMIT ENTERTAINMENT

GILLIAN BOHRER, VICE PRESIDENT, PRODUCTION, SUMMIT ENTERTAINMENT

ANDI ISAACS, EXECUTIVE VICE PRESIDENT AND HEAD OF PHYSICAL PRODUCTION,
SUMMIT ENTERTAINMENT

All around us, my friends and neighbors and petty enemies ate and laughed and swayed to the music, oblivious to the fact that they were about to face horror, danger, maybe death.

Because of me.[1]

the twilight saga
eclipse

THE OFFICIAL ILLUSTRATED MOVIE COMPANION

BY MARK COTTA VAZ

atom

ATOM

Motion Picture Artwork TM & © 2010 by Summit Entertainment, LLC,
unless otherwise credited
Text copyright © 2010 by Little, Brown and Company
Complete work copyright © Summit Entertainment, LLC, and Little, Brown and Company

A CIP catalogue record for this book
is available from the British Library.

First Atom UK edition 2010

Book design by Georgia Rucker Design

ISBN 978-1-907410-00-0

Printed and bound in the UK by Butler Tanner & Dennis Ltd, Frome

Atom
An imprint of
Little, Brown Book Group
100 Victoria Embankment
London EC4Y 0DY

An Hachette UK Company
www.hachette.co.uk

www.atombooks.co.uk

TABLE OF CONTENTS

INTRODUCTION

E•CLIPSE (i-KLIPS): **1. to cause an eclipse of; darken or obscure
2. to obscure the fame or glory of; overshadow; out-shine; surpass.**

—*WEBSTER'S NEW WORLD DICTIONARY*

Icy droplets spattered against my face as the rain began to fall.

It was too dark to see much besides the black triangles of the spruces leaning and shaking with the wind. But I strained my eyes anyway, searching for other shapes in the storm. A pale silhouette, moving like a ghost through the black . . . or maybe the shadowy outline of an enormous wolf. . . . My eyes were too weak.

Then there was a movement in the night, right beside me. Edward slid through my open window, his hands colder than the rain.

"Is Jacob out there?" I asked, shivering as Edward pulled me into the circle of his arm.

"Yes . . . somewhere."

—FROM STEPHENIE MEYER'S *ECLIPSE*[2]

Gathering Shadows

On a rainy night in Seattle, Washington, a figure pauses under an awning before stepping into the downpour. The streets are dark and deserted, but what quickens the step and chills the heart is an ominous shadow swooping in like the filmy reflection of a living nightmare. The shadow chases its prey to a dead end on the waterfront, and its teeth leave a crescent-moon-shaped bite mark that takes the victim's humanity, leaving a newly born vampire.

A thrill for fans, this sequence sets up one of the scenes written for *The Twilight Saga: Eclipse*, the third film adaptation of Stephenie Meyer's bestselling THE TWILIGHT SAGA novels. Although Meyer's books unfold through the first-person perspective of Bella Swan, the high school student who dreams of being with her vampire boyfriend, Edward Cullen, for eternity, the victim in the film's opening scene is college student Riley Biers, who has been changed by Victoria. The red-haired and vicious Victoria still seeks revenge upon Edward and Bella for the death of her mate.

Riley becomes Victoria's tool to pluck fresh victims from the streets of Seattle to create a rampaging army of newborn vampires to descend on the town of Forks, Washington, and take vengeance on Bella and the Cullen clan. The creation of the newborns, which happened out of Bella's sight in the shadows of the novel, provided the filmmakers with an opportunity to enlarge on Meyer's mythology.

"In the first two movies, we've been appropriately slavish in having everything intimately seen from Bella's point of view," noted Melissa Rosenberg, screenwriter for all the film adaptations of THE TWILIGHT SAGA. "But for *Eclipse*, we got to go away from Bella's perspective a couple times, to explore some of the outside world in the context of the mythology."

"Since the books were written from Bella's point of view, anything that she doesn't see, or get told about, you don't know," observed *The Twilight Saga: Eclipse* director David Slade. "Part of our job as filmmakers was to imagine that stuff, which we did in close contact with Stephenie Meyer. The thing is, all these events, whether they've been written down in the novels or not, have taken place. How did Victoria and Riley meet, for example? Stephenie was amazing, in that she always knew what had happened."

As with the first two productions, *The Twilight Saga: Eclipse* would be faithful to the book, which raised the stakes for the romantic triangle of Bella, Edward, and Jacob Black, the

Xavier Samuel as Riley Biers.

Kristen Stewart as Bella Swan and Taylor Lautner as Jacob Black.

teenage Quileute with the ability to "phase" into a werewolf. "The first film was about establishing the *Twilight* world and Bella being introduced to Edward," Slade said. "*New Moon* was about dealing with Bella's conflicted emotions about Jacob. *Eclipse* is about how complicated this world is *now*. As a result, the characters have to be more mature, the story is more mature. The decisions characters make in each scene will lead to life-or-death consequences."

"In the course of the film, Bella hears the stories of Rosalie and Jasper, spends time with her parents and friends—realizing she will have to say goodbye to them—and comes to terms with her real feelings for Jacob and the happy life she would undoubtedly

"Eclipse IS ABOUT HOW COMPLICATED THIS WORLD IS *now*."

have with him," said Summit vice president of production Gillian Bohrer. "Bella is forced to confront the realities of her choice. She can't have it all, but she can—with eyes wide open—choose the life she wants."

The Twilight Saga: Eclipse had a hard act to follow. *The Twilight Saga: New Moon*, released on November 20, 2009, had dramatically raised the profile of Summit Entertainment's franchise. *Twilight* had been a smash hit, with almost $400 million in worldwide box office, but *New Moon* almost doubled that—by mid-January 2010, the domestic box office topped $290 million, and the international box office was over $410 million, a staggering return for a production reportedly budgeted at

Bella (Stewart) visits her mom (Sarah Clarke) in Florida.

$50 million. "*The Twilight Saga* franchise has been an incredible ride and we at Summit have always believed in the power of the characters and story that Stephenie Meyer created," said Summit co-chairman and chief executive officer Rob Friedman. "Translating these elements to film has been a wonderful challenge and we are pleased that with the second film we were able to grow the audience and fan base for *The Twilight Saga.*"

But box office numbers were just a way of keeping score. The studio and the filmmakers were riding the wave of a pop culture phenomenon. "Twilighters" (one of the names bestowed upon the fervent fans) were a presence, both in the virtual realm of Internet blogs and fan sites, and on location—in the Portland, Oregon, area, where *Twilight* filmed during one of the worst winters in years, and on *The Twilight Saga: New Moon* sites, includ-

ing the production's base in the Canadian city of Vancouver, British Columbia, and the medieval cobblestone streets of Montepulciano, in the Tuscany region of Italy.

Indeed, as the first decade of the twenty-first century drew to a close, vampires were shining in the pop culture firmament. In the wake of the first two wildly successful film adaptations of THE TWILIGHT SAGA, vampire-oriented material included the television shows *The Vampire Diaries* and *True Blood* and feature films such as *Daybreakers*. In fact, in 2007 David Slade had followed up his first feature, the 2005 release *Hard Candy*, with his own vampire epic, *30 Days of Night*, based on a graphic novel about a pack of feral vampires who descend on a remote Alaskan town during its seasonal thirty days without sunlight.

Slade would be the third director for *The Twilight Saga* franchise. After the success of

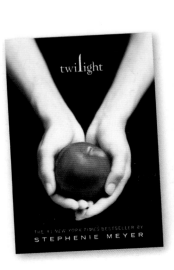

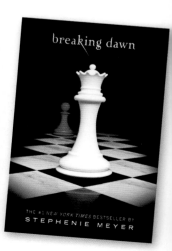

the first film, released on November 21, 2008, Summit quickly scheduled the second for theatrical release the following November. The production time line shrank even further with the June 30, 2010, release date for *Eclipse*. It created a revolving door, with preproduction on the next film beginning even as the previous film was in postproduction. It was physically impossible for one director to juggle two productions simultaneously. Summit Entertainment also determined that each of Meyer's books had its own distinctive atmosphere and story line, and it made sense to match the material with the appropriate director.

"*Twilight* is raw and real and Catherine Hardwicke was the first director I met with and the only director for that movie," Summit president of production Erik Feig has noted. "*New Moon* has more complicated emotions, with bigger forces at work, and Chris Weitz was the director with the skill to show that. On *Eclipse*, the challenge is, how do you visualize and show an audience that a choice has consequences and that Bella is in a crucible of multiple decisions and options? Who can get that? David Slade."[3]

"Director David Slade was the perfect choice," said Summit co-chairman and president Patrick Wachsberger. "He brought to the production a sharp visual sense and an edge to the storytelling that parallels what is going on in the lives of Bella, Edward, Jacob, and all the other characters that make up *Eclipse*."

Producer Wyck Godfrey was intrigued with Slade after seeing the director's low-budget independent debut feature. *Hard Candy* tells the story of a teenage girl who connects with an older man online and then holds him captive in his house to exact revenge for the dark secrets of his past. Although far from the gothic romance of Bella and Edward, that movie made Godfrey want to hire Slade for *Eclipse*.

"In *Hard Candy*, David really accessed [Ellen Page's] abilities and did a great job telling the story from the point of view of a teenage girl. In his next film, *30 Days of Night*, David demonstrated how well he could handle intense, frightening action. While *Eclipse*, like the rest of *The Twilight Saga*, is told from Bella's point of view, it's also a much darker and more dangerous movie than *New Moon*. Given David's unique mix of talents, he was the perfect choice."

For Godfrey, selecting the right director was just the first step in the process of assembling a film crew. "Being a producer is like being a

> "*Eclipse* IS A MUCH DARKER AND MORE DANGEROUS MOVIE THAN *New Moon*."

coach of a football team, where your job is to recruit the best players. The director is basically the quarterback, the player on the field who makes it all happen. But just as a quarterback might be better suited to a certain receiver or running back, you have to find [department heads and crew members who] play to the strength of the director.

"We ended up keeping Javier Aguirresarobe, our director of photography [DP] for *The Twilight Saga: New Moon*, because David Slade really liked his work. Then David had a production designer he had worked with, Paul Austerberry, and the shorthand they had developed helped David, who was being thrown into this machine that had already been built."

Austerberry, who had worked with Slade on *30 Days of Night*, noted that the vampire worlds of the two films were like night and day. "The vampires [from *30 Days*] are feral and vicious."

Meyer's vampire mythology isn't based on the classic malevolent night stalkers who perish in sunlight and must crawl into their coffins before daybreak. In the world of THE TWILIGHT SAGA, vampires don't sleep, and direct sunlight makes their skin sparkle. Thus, the year-round rainy and cloudy weather in Forks suits Bella's friends, the Cullens, a clan of "vegetarian vampires" who feast on animals instead of humans and who wish to blend in with human society.

The third novel brought to the foreground a new aspect of Meyer's innovative vampire mythology—the idea that humans who have been freshly transformed into vampires are violent creatures who can't control their blood-thirsty urges. ECLIPSE also revealed legendary secrets about the shape-shifting Quileute tribe and what it meant for the young wolf pack of the present and their uneasy truce with the

The Cullens head to the woods to prepare for battle.

vampire world. The possibilities of translating all that and more into the movie medium excited the production principals, cast, and crew.

As Slade entered THE TWILIGHT SAGA world, screenwriter Melissa Rosenberg was already deep into creating that blueprint. It would be Slade's first task when he came aboard to help "break" the story.

The intense production schedule for the films was a whirlwind, and Melissa Rosenberg was caught up in it, even as she was busy with her other full-time job, as an executive producer and the head writer for the Showtime television series *Dexter*. *Twilight* had not yet appeared in theaters when Rosenberg was writing the screenplay for *New Moon* from June through October 2008—and then *Eclipse* loomed.

"I meant to jump onto *Eclipse*, but I was so burnt," Rosenberg recalled. "I piddled around on it; I wasn't being productive. Then the new year came around, and I realized I had to slam on this thing. When I read the third book, I had thought it would be an easy one; it has a lot of action. But all the action really happens in the last chunk of the book and the last twenty minutes of the movie. When I started breaking down the story—oh, man! It was the hardest of the three!"

As with any film adaptation of a literary work, much of the screenwriter's challenge was making the story and the characters work on the screen. The screenplay sometimes required going beyond what was in the novels, to what Rosenberg calls "invention." An example of invention in *The Twilight Saga: New Moon* was the fight scene in the Volturi's inner sanctum between Edward and Felix, the vampire guard.

"For that little tableau with the Volturi, there was never a big fight in the book,

The Volturi keep an eye on developing events.

although the confrontation was there—I just took it to the next level," Rosenberg explained. "So much of what I do when translating a book to a movie is to take things one step further. As a screenwriter, you have to take what is in the book, such as internal thoughts and conversation, and externalize it, make it visually exciting. It's about heightening every confrontation and making things more visual and intense, a lot of which comes from condensing a book and taking something that one step further. It's a visual medium, so you have to make things cinematic.

"By *Eclipse*, I'd gotten more comfortable and confident in this world. I wasn't bound by Bella's perspective, so I got to show things she only heard about after the fact in the novel, such as when the Cullens and [the] wolves chase Victoria. I could develop things hidden between the lines in the book. I have Riley, for example, be from Forks, which is why Victoria chose him. There was also reorganizing things, such as flashback stories of Jasper and Rosalie, which happen in different places in the film than in the book. Since there was so much invention going on, I

"IT'S ABOUT HEIGHTENING EVERY CONFRONTATION AND MAKING THINGS MORE VISUAL AND INTENSE."

was concerned I wasn't violating Stephenie's mythology."

The screenwriter in Southern California and the author in Arizona usually brainstormed via long-distance phone conversations. "The hardest part of writing any script is breaking the story, and I do a very detailed, twenty- to twenty-five-page single-spaced outline," Rosenberg added.

By the time Slade was on board, Rosenberg was on a second draft and began tailoring it to the director. It was a creative process that fed both of them, with Slade developing storyboards that informed, and were informed by, Rosenberg's evolving script. "I started tailoring the screenplay to him," Rosenberg explained, "and he would enhance and sharpen it in whatever direction he wanted. For example, in the opening sequence, Riley is fearful he's going to get bit, so I had him running down a street to the water's edge. David loved the idea of Victoria as a shadow, and he built on that sequence in his storyboards. . . . He would talk me through the storyboards, and I would put that in the script. It was the perfect collaboration."

Slade brought a finely honed sensibility,

"I think Melissa was very much at the center of saying, 'For *Eclipse*, let's see the newborns, let's see what's going on in Seattle.' That was ultimately a very smart decision, because it provided the danger through the first half of the movie, which you might not have felt otherwise."

—WYCK GODFREY, PRODUCER

Godfrey on set.

Riley sets about creating an army.

"Bella doesn't know what's going on with Riley when he's not in her presence. So, although Stephenie can't put that in, the mythology is much more complex than what actually goes on the page. I'm always nervous about pitching a screenplay idea to an author, as it's their child, but Stephenie is very flexible and had a lot of ideas. She was very helpful while I was writing the screenplay."

—MELISSA ROSENBERG, SCREENWRITER

"It was a whirlwind, just a couple weeks from the first phone call to working on the script. The entire project was hard and fast, with a set start and wrap date along with a set-in-stone release date. It was going to be a leap into the abyss. The book seemed too vast to fit into a film. Jasper's story and the origins of the Quileute tribe's shape-shifting ability seemed to warrant their own films. But Melissa's script convinced me that it could work by centering on Bella and Edward's story and all the consequences of the choice to exit her human life for an immortal one. *Eclipse* is grounded in the emotional maturing that leads to Bella's concrete choice."

—DAVID SLADE, DIRECTOR

David Slade grew up in the midlands of England and was on a career path as a writer and journalist when he swerved into the world of visual media.

"My primary focus was to tell stories, but as I had a strong visual sense, I decided to develop in that direction," Slade explained. "My world changed direction when I went to Sheffield Polytechnic [now Sheffield Hallam University] to study for a fine arts degree, rather than further a more concrete career in journalism. This was three years of transformation, moonlighting at the Sheffield Independent Film unit, a community center for people wanting to learn about film.

"I traded time with equipment and technical advice for work time repairing disassembled editing suites and cutting rooms during the weekends, which I spent making my own short films, video art installation pieces, and other experiments with the various forms of the moving image available to me. I would work with videotape when I couldn't afford film, operate a one-man crew when it came to the work I would produce, sometimes finish special effects using early computer graphics [CG]. All of this led to a self-taught, hands-on approach to film-making I have retained to this day."

knowledge, and history to the not-so-simple act of reading *The Twilight Saga: Eclipse* screenplay. "Reading a script is emotionally exhausting for me; it's not about looking at words on a page. All of the mechanics of cinema become second nature and kind of inhabit your brain, so when you pick up a screenplay, all those tools are there. I see not just pictures in my head I have to translate into a scene, but pictures in cinematic terms. The film unfolds in your mind; that's how it starts. You know what you're going to need, but the most exciting part is when you don't know and have to figure it out. You don't come at it all at once, because it becomes overwhelming. You break the story down in pieces to understand it.

"In this production, Stephenie Meyer became the lead, really. I was lucky enough to work with Melissa Rosenberg and Stephenie

"EACH FILM IN THE SERIES HAS ITS OWN EXCLUSIVE SIGNATURE."

during the script development. There's the technical side and the aesthetic side, for sure, but what really drives a film is character and story. You figure out the point of view of the film, and then you start building your arsenal. The acting is part of the cinematography, part of the drive in lighting, and part of the drive in the special effects."

It was shortly after principal photography for *New Moon* wrapped in June 2009 that *Eclipse* began. When Slade arrived at the production offices in Vancouver, *New Moon* had transitioned to editing, visual effects, the musical score, and other postproduction challenges.

"Based on both the story's progression and the success of the first two films in the series, we knew we needed to take our filmmaking and production to another level," said Friedman. "The story grows increasingly complicated and the audience commitment to the characters is further realized, and thus the production value needed to keep pace."

Co-producer Bill Bannerman recalls that after giving the company time off to recharge, they "hit the ground running" for *Eclipse*. Bannerman, who described his job as "on-site construction foreman," was in charge of logistics and making sure that once filming began, production stayed on time and on budget so that it could wrap by Halloween of 2009.

"My crew was a little larger than what we had on *New Moon*," Bannerman said. "We were building sets on three different soundstages at once, which included construction and set decoration, and we had the infrastructure for the main-office crew. We also had our main unit and second unit, which were working simultaneously for about seventy percent of the schedule. It varied from week to week, but the aggregate was six hundred to eight hundred people. It was quite a group."

Integral to the look was returning DP Javier Aguirresarobe, who brought back his *New Moon* crew, including gaffer Owen Taylor and grip John Westerlaken. The camera-and-lighting department used the same basic tools as the previous production, including Panavision cameras and lenses. Since the production was shooting in late summer, Aguirresarobe found himself having to use more silks and cloths to soften or shield the sun when filming vampire characters under ostensibly overcast skies.

"I think each film in the series has its own exclusive signature," Aguirresarobe noted. "The style of *New Moon* was very different from that of *Twilight*, or at least that was the intention of Chris Weitz and myself. David Slade wanted *Eclipse* to have its own singular look. To achieve this, he used elements not often employed in the previous productions, such as a regular use of long focal lenses, the use of the dolly for camera movements, and an exceptional use of the Steadicam. David Slade's visual and aesthetic perception is a very demanding one. For *Eclipse*, he proposed working with different tonalities of color depending on the different scenes and situations, though he would usually choose warm tones. It was all of these parameters together that allowed for a cinematographic approach exclusive to this production."

"David Slade is a storyteller, but he is also a stylist—he uses a lot of the tools in the toolbox," added Eric Leven, visual effects supervisor for Tippett Studio, the visual effects house that reprised its werewolf work from *The Twilight Saga: New Moon*. "He'll use [digital] color techniques to bring out contrast. He'll tell a story just by compressing space and using a longer lens rather than just rely on an actor's performance."

The crew rigged up cloths to simulate overcast skies for filming.

Stewart practices a punch with Lautner on set.

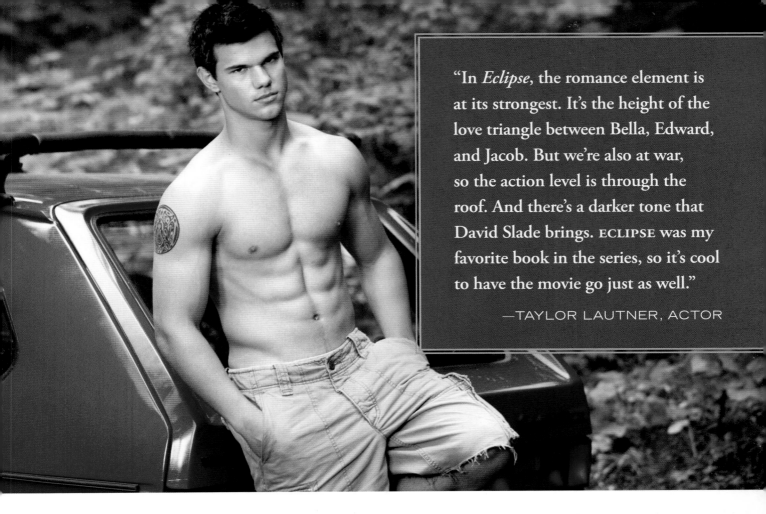

"In *Eclipse*, the romance element is at its strongest. It's the height of the love triangle between Bella, Edward, and Jacob. But we're also at war, so the action level is through the roof. And there's a darker tone that David Slade brings. ECLIPSE was my favorite book in the series, so it's cool to have the movie go just as well."

—TAYLOR LAUTNER, ACTOR

The lighting-and-camera work went hand in hand with the color scheme and even the sets that production designer Austerberry and his art department designed and built. "The first film was bluish in color, quite a cool color palette, and there was a decision to warm it up a bit for the second film," Austerberry said. "We also had the same DP, and David agreed to continue along those lines of a slightly warmer palette. Of course, there was nothing for us to copy from Chris Weitz's film, because when we began our production, that film was still being edited. But there were three basic color schemes for *Eclipse*. The Cullens are all cool blue with warm accents. The Quileute Nation and the hot-blooded werewolves have red accents all through their palette: Jacob's car is red, Jacob's house is red, the pickup truck

Jacob's dad gave Bella is red. The third palette is the people of Forks, which is a mixed palette of earthy, warm colors."

Although the design changed to suit each movie, the series has consistent iconic locations, such as the house where Bella lived with her father, Charlie. It was a real house in the Portland area that had been used for *Twilight* and faithfully re-created as an outdoor set when the production shifted to Vancouver for *The Twilight Saga: New Moon*.

"*Eclipse*, as the third in a series, had established locations and looks, which I more or less had to adhere to," Austerberry said. "You're not quite as free, but sometimes you can have too much freedom, which can be a lot harder than having some constraints. In addition to talking

The Swan house.

to David Slade, I'd also check in with Stephenie Meyer because certain colors and descriptions in her books also affected the design."

There would be plenty for the production design and art department to dream up and for the construction department to build. In addition to period flashbacks for the Quileute legend and Jasper's and Rosalie's stories, sets included a meticulous re-creation of the original Cullen house and a mountaintop sound-stage set for the final face-off between Victoria and Riley and Edward.

Binding it all together to create the "singular look" that Aguirresarobe alluded to was an accent on realism. Image Engine, a Vancouver-based visual effects house, came onto the production on the strength of such recent work as *District 9*, for which the group created computer-generated extraterrestrials. "David Slade connected with the raw nature and gritty sensibility and documentary style of *District 9*," said Image Engine visual effects executive producer Shawn Walsh. "He was looking to bring a gritty sensibility to the *Twilight* series, based on this particular novel. He felt that some of what we had accomplished on *District 9* could be used in the mix of creating a visceral, real feeling for *Eclipse*."

Overseeing the visual effects effort was a department on the production side that

"WHAT HAPPENS WHEN A VAMPIRE GETS HIS ARM TORN OFF?"

included several supervisors, producers, and coordinators. "It's always a balance between staying true to what has gone before, both in the books and on the screen, and making each film with the creative imprimatur of a unique director," reflected production visual effects coordinator Jeremy Ball. "Because visual effects are so integral to the supernatural elements of the story, there is a lot more room for interpretation. What happens when a vampire gets his arm torn off, for example? There are guidelines in the books, but every director is going to come at it with a slightly different approach for how something should be realized visually. There isn't an objective reality you can point to in this world to say, 'This is how it is.' Things can shift from installment to installment."

"There were challenges in translating the immense amount of supernatural lore into an emotionally powerful drama," Slade noted. "However, in reading the book and the script, I felt these things had to unfold in a believable way. This meant not stretching the boundaries of physics too far, keeping performances as subtle as you would in any drama. When I sat down with the actors, I told them we were going for a more mature approach, because the characters are becoming more mature. As a result, the smart thing was for everything to follow suit—for the special effects to be as invisible as possible, that any computer work be carefully designed to fit in seamlessly. The motivation for all of that was story-driven; it was all about the complexity of this world."

THERE WOULD BE
PLENTY FOR THE
PRODUCTION DESIGN
AND ART DEPARTMENT
TO DREAM UP AND FOR
THE CONSTRUCTION
DEPARTMENT TO BUILD.

*The set created for
the Quileute village.*

*The meticulous set re-creation
of the house used for the
Cullen home in Twilight.*

*The incredible
snowy mountaintop
soundstage set.*

"The big difference for Edward in the last two movies was he lived in a very isolated way; he's been aloof from the world. Now that he's in a real relationship with Bella, he has to become part of the real world. In a way, he has to become more human."

—ROBERT PATTINSON, ACTOR

*Edward (Robert Pattinson)
and Bella (Kristen Stewart)
visit their favorite meadow.*

"One of the themes of this movie is about how unconditional love gets tested.
Bella and Edward are undeniably devoted to each other, but they're more open;
they talk more. They're willing to let more people into their lives and not just
have this exclusive relationship."

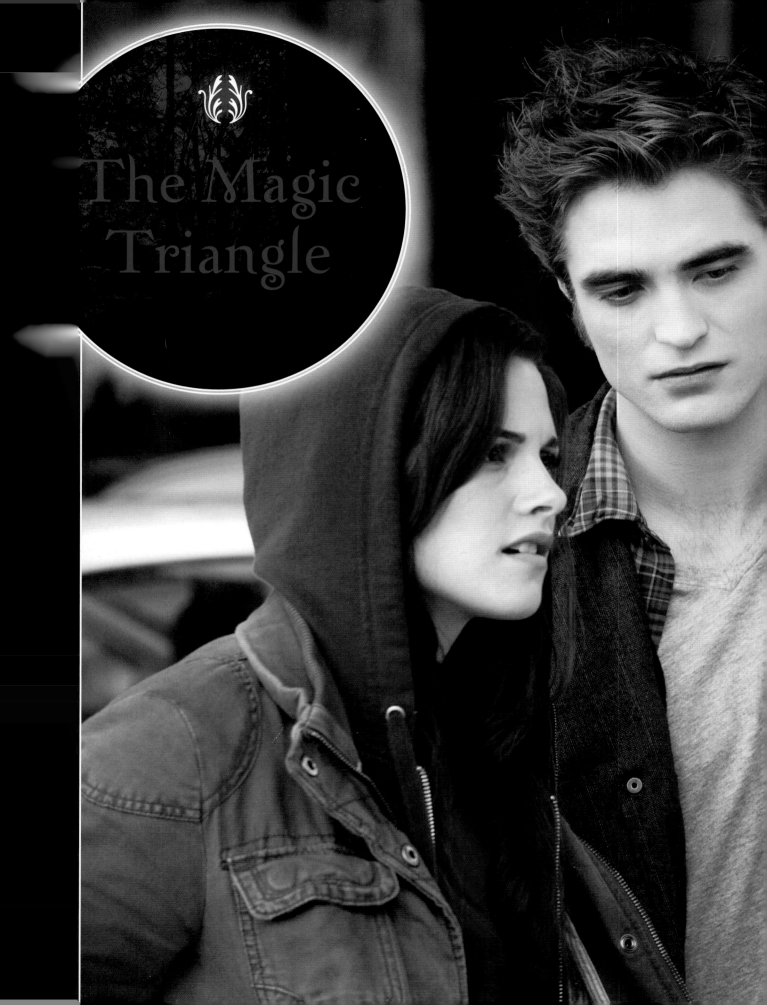

The Magic Triangle

Kristen Stewart as Bella Swan,
Robert Pattinson as Edward Cullen,
and Taylor Lautner as Jacob Black.

As many enraptured fans know, THE TWILIGHT SAGA is a love story at heart. Bella Swan, a seventeen-year-old, falls in love with a classmate who happens to be a vampire, while a younger male friend who carries a torch for her is revealed to be able to transform into a werewolf. By the time of ECLIPSE, the proverbial cards are on the table—at the end of NEW MOON, Edward asks Bella to marry him, even as Jacob tells Bella he loves her and is prepared to challenge Edward to win her.

"[The film] *New Moon* was more character-driven and about developing the characters and relationships of what we call the 'magic triangle' of Bella, Jacob, and Edward," noted Bill Bannerman, the line producer on *New Moon*, who was back on *Eclipse* with a co-producer credit. "When I read ECLIPSE, I got extremely excited.

Each book is like a new chapter in this unfolding story, and each one ramps up character development and action. That's great for the movies, because your appetite as a moviegoer wants more and the story serves you. *Eclipse* sort of multiplied things by a factor of six in intensity and detail, because it required a complex chess game of action that comes into play in the second and third acts."

"The fun of writing *The Twilight Saga* films is that triangle," Melissa Rosenberg said. Although *Eclipse* is darker and more violent than the other films, the "love story is still front and center," noted Wyck Godfrey, whose focus as producer was to make sure each production maintained continuity and was faithful to the books and the previous films.

"It's been fantastic to see how Kristen

[Stewart], Robert [Pattinson], and Taylor [Lautner] have deftly handled the evolution of their characters over the first three films," Godfrey observed. "In *Twilight*, Bella is deeply insecure, fearing that she's not worthy of Edward's love. By *Eclipse*, Bella no longer questions whether she's good enough for Edward, but rather whether Edward is right for her. She's forced to ask herself this, because Jacob has finally gained the confidence to show Bella how he truly feels and present her with a real alternative. As a result, Bella finds herself torn—does she become a vampire and risk losing her friendship with Jacob? Or does she choose a human life with Jacob, where she can grow old and have children?"

For David Slade, rehearsals were key to the actors' performances, building the ensemble one

"I told the actors, 'You know who you are and what you've done—but you're evolving.' All the questions an actor has, all the challenges of the story, can change a character. Edward is different from *Twilight* to *Eclipse* via *New Moon*—he's even different at the beginning of *Eclipse* from the character you meet at the end of *Eclipse*. That's a process of understanding text and point of view and all the little facets of the story, and that's before it gets to camera. If I give a direction, it's a case of *why* and then *because*. All of those things add up, and eventually they make the performance you see on the screen."

—DAVID SLADE, DIRECTOR

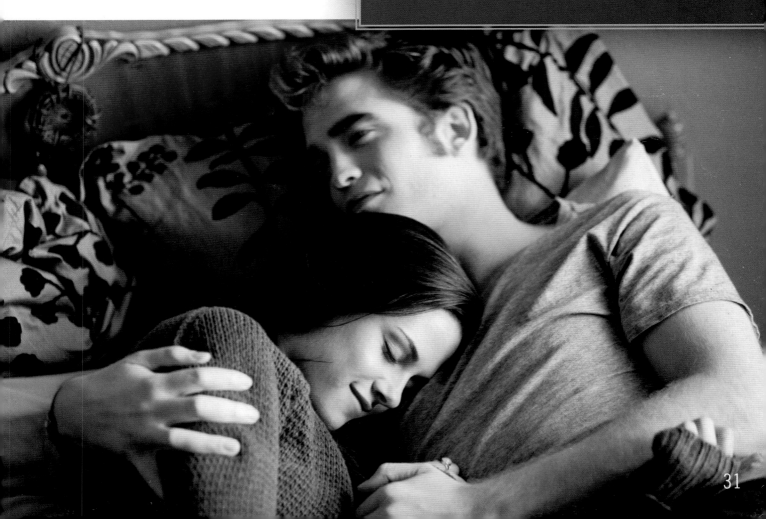

Director Slade talks to Stewart and Lautner on set.

actor at a time. "You take away all the cinematic veils, all the technical stuff. I like to meet with actors individually, so it's not just everyone coming to a common text but everyone coming to a common text with a point of view. Everyone has questions, answers are given, and they go do their preparation. Then, in the ensemble, everybody brings their own take. That's the trade secret of breaking a story and characters and making sure each character shines.

"The Cullen family alone is an ensemble, and for each of them to retain an identity, you have to address the individual pieces. That's the rehearsal process, notes, and homework. Some actors want detailed notes; others just need a general direction. Everybody

"ROSALIE'S HARD SHELL CRACKS A LITTLE BIT, AND YOU GET TO SEE INSIDE HER CHARACTER."

is different, but it's all appropriate. In this case, these actors really know their characters because they've inhabited them for two previous films, which was gratifying on a fifty-day shooting schedule with little prep time. I was like, 'What do *you* want? What can I give to *you*?'

"All of the characters and, to a degree, some of the villains are heroic," Slade continued. "The wolf pack of young Quileutes that were so mysterious in *New Moon* become clearer in *Eclipse*. You learn the tribe's history and see that they represent a noble and heroic position. To me, the Cullen family [members] are a metaphor for how things traditionally viewed as bad or even evil can actually be positive and heroic. Jasper, in this film, emerges as a tactical player. Rosalie's hard shell cracks a little bit, and you get to see inside her character.

"Charlie, Bella's father, is heroic—he consoles and comforts, he cares, he's a support mechanism for Bella. But in *Eclipse*, Bella has guilt

32

that she will be saying goodbye forever to her father [by becoming a vampire]. Charlie, in turn, is antagonizing that guilt by being a great father!

"As a character, Charlie is inherently comedic, but at the same time he can also tear at your heartstrings, thanks to the great skills of [actor] Billy Burke. We'd say, 'You can never have enough Billy Burke, you can never have enough Charlie.' Charlie just works; Charlie is magical. But they are all smartly designed and functioning characters in this story. The function of an ensemble is multifaceted, and everybody pulls and pushes."

Although screenwriter Melissa Rosenberg had fun writing the romantic triangle, she admitted it was a challenge writing the confrontation scenes between Edward and Jacob. After all, Jacob was a teen, while Edward had been around since 1901.

"With those two actors, there's a lot of heat there, but having them confront each other was harder than you might think," Rosenberg mused. "You don't want Edward to be petulant

> "Billy Burke is such a wonderful actor, whenever he's on-screen the whole thing becomes so grounded in reality. He's extraordinarily talented, and the relationship his character has with Bella is so rich, and I love tracking that and writing toward it. The leads are fun, but some of the secondary characters, particularly as played by these actors, are really rich and fun to write."
>
> —MELISSA ROSENBERG, SCREENWRITER

and trading insults, because he's been around for more than a hundred years and, with Jacob, it's like he's dealing with a child. But Edward is also experiencing the primal emotion of jealousy, which is beyond age. The big challenge was

The much-anticipated confrontation during the "sleeping bag" scene.

"I like to think Charlie is the passageway to reality for these movies, in addition to maybe being a bit of the moral compass. He's there to keep his daughter grounded and safe and, hopefully, happy."

—BILLY BURKE, ACTOR

Charlie Swan (Billy Burke) with his daughter, Bella (Kristen Stewart).

writing and rewriting so their conversation did not devolve into an exchange of insults.

"In my early drafts, I was going to town with that stuff, with Edward telling Jacob he had no control and could accidentally kill anyone, alluding to what Sam did to Emily and that he could do that to Bella. At that point, it became a question of why Edward was even engaging in this way."

Director of photography Javier Aguirresarobe had his own challenges in visually capturing the romantic tension. "I tried to follow the same guidelines with Edward as with Jacob in the romantic scenes with Bella," Aguirresarobe said. "I didn't find any real motives to make me create different atmospheres in the sequences where they contend for Bella's love. Perhaps Bella's declared love for Edward and their closer relationship led me to use more sensual color tones and contrasts in their more intimate scenes together.

"With Jacob and Edward, I didn't want to exaggerate, photographically, their confrontation. I placed my trust in the excellence of their acting when both actors challenged each other. I was possibly influenced by Bella's philosophy of wanting to maintain in good harmony her friendship with Jacob."

The confrontation scenes were of special concern to costume designer Tish Monaghan. Although Edward had the requisite speed and superstrength of a vampire, he looked lean and pale compared to Jacob. "Robert, as an actor, wanted to make sure his character could stand up as a visual foe of Jacob, who is strong and

muscular and goes around without a shirt on," Monaghan observed. "So I gave him a little dimension, with layers. While there's a lot more outward physicality to Jacob and how he stakes out his territory, Edward maintains his ground in a quieter way that's just as strong. It's an Edward Cullen stance."

Monaghan was another of the production department heads from *The Twilight Saga: New Moon* who returned for the third film. Just a few weeks earlier, Monaghan and a six-person crew had been in the walled city of Montepulciano, preparing more than 900 costumes, including some 850 red-hooded cloaks, for the dramatic procession that fills the city square as Bella rushes to stop Edward from stepping into the sunlight. Monaghan recalled finishing her *New Moon* work on May 28, 2009. By June 14, she was on *Eclipse* until the production wrapped in October. It was, she noted, a "continuum," not only in her own transition to the new production but in the story itself, with *Eclipse* picking up where *New Moon* left off.

"It was already a comfortable slot to move into," Monaghan noted. "I did have an interview with the new director, and we had a great meeting. The production [team] was also pleased with what I had done on *New Moon*. David Slade was willing to go along with [the general look of the established costumes], and we also had discussions about new characters. But for me it was comforting to deal with a cast of characters I had already established a direction for, although we did go off in slight variations for the Cullens and Bella."

Those "slight variations" were problematic,

"We've been living with these characters for a while now, so we're starting to get used to them, learn about them, and actually adapt to them.

"In this movie I need to rough up Edward a bit, but Rob is too likable. [*laughs*] We'll be laughing and joking around before the take, but when 'Action!' is called, all of a sudden I've got to get into a mode—*I hate this guy!*"

—TAYLOR LAUTNER, ACTOR

given there was no significant passage of time between any of the films. "Realistically, would Bella have gone out and bought a new wardrobe?" the costume designer rhetorically asked. "The truth is, no, she wouldn't. The fact was, the cast members and costume department were tired of those clothes!" Monaghan said, laughing. "We bought her a completely new closet [of clothes], although it's just a slight variation of what she has worn. The story line was also moving from a fall-winter-spring picture to late spring and summer. So I felt we were able to give Kristen new clothes while respecting the things established in the previous movies, a bit more jeans and T-shirts."

Costume design for Edward Cullen meant going back to the character's roots. For most of *The Twilight Saga: New Moon*, he had been dressed in the gray tweed suit he wore for Bella's eighteenth-birthday party, that fateful gathering at the Cullen house in which Bella cut herself and triggered Jasper's bloodlust, which led to Edward's decision to leave her. With *The Twilight Saga: Eclipse*, Edward was back in Forks and, along with Bella and their classmates, looking forward to graduation from Forks High School.

"Edward primarily wore a suit in *New Moon*, and by the time we saw him in Italy, his suit was in a state of disrepair," Monaghan noted. "I wanted to put him back in the world of a twelfth-grade student, to make sure the audience understood he was still a high school student. He's now in jeans, T-shirts and button-up shirts, casual jackets, and he had a hoodie as an homage to Bella. I also had pulled a jean jacket out for Robert, and I wasn't pushing it at him, but he put it on and he looked great! With

"[Bella and Edward] want the same things from each other; they just have different ways of expressing it."

—KRISTEN STEWART, ACTRESS

"Jacob needed to be a legitimate rival, and Rob had to play this feeling of jealousy from someone who has been around for over a hundred years. That was an interesting balance, and one of the bigger challenges."
—MELISSA ROSENBERG, SCREENWRITER

that jacket and T-shirt, he had a cool, James Dean–type look. It was a little bit of a departure, a more casual look for his character."

Integral to transforming the actors into their characters was Gina Sherritt, who had worked in *The Twilight Saga: New Moon* hair department as "right-hand gal" to key hairstylist Thom McIntyre.

During *Eclipse* actress Kristen Stewart had cut her hair short and dyed it black for another movie. "So we made three wigs for Kristen that matched the earlier look for Bella," Sherritt explained.

Elizabeth Reaser as Esme Cullen and Peter Facinelli as Dr. Carlisle Cullen.

"On second unit, we had to match the first unit. Sometimes you don't know how long an actor will have to sit around on set in their makeup [before they have to go before camera], so in the makeup trailer I like to sketch things in first and then do the detail work when I'm on set, like getting close to the eyes and making sure everything is perfect.

"Some actors get into character as the makeup goes on; their persona changes. Then I've seen actors who can be laughing and joking around, and the instant they say 'Action,' they're in character. They can turn it on in a flash."

—JOANN FOWLER, MAKEUP LEAD, SECOND UNIT

Vampires, whether sophisticated Cullens or raging newborns, wouldn't really be vampires without their pale, porcelain skin, and for the movies that means makeup. Charles Porlier headed the main-unit makeup department, with first assistants Patricia Murray, Lise Kuhr, and Michelle Hrescak. The makeup lead on the second unit was JoAnn Fowler, who had as her first assistants Amy St. Jean, Ceilidh Dunn, and Amber Trudeau.

The second unit is an integral part of moviemaking. While a director and a cinematographer work with actors on the major scenes, the second unit typically handles stunts and action, pickup scenes, sequences delegated by the director, and generally all the pieces needed to augment the main unit's work. On *The Twilight Saga: Eclipse*, the second unit, which the production called the "action unit," had particular importance, given the many action scenes that required not only the usual complement of stunt performers and extras but also the star actors. "We had a lot of cast on our unit," explained JoAnn Fowler, who had also done makeup on both units for *New Moon*. "There was a lot of action to do, including scenes of the Cullens training to fight the newborns, and the battle itself."

Before filming began in the middle of August, Fowler worked with Porlier for three weeks of prep, which involved everything from selecting the makeup products to doing camera tests and establishing continuity. The makeup philosophy for the vampires of *Eclipse*, Fowler explained, was to not pick one product for everyone but to make each performer's makeup a little different, particularly since newborns were different nationalities. "*Eclipse* tried to keep the integrity of the look and level of whiteness for the vampires that [makeup designer] Norma Hill-Patton established in *New Moon*," Fowler explained.

The second unit handled a lot of vampires. Normal workdays began at three o'clock in the morning to get the performers ready by seven. There would be up to thirty vampires, by Fowler's estimates. While the makeup artists on *Eclipse* got a chance to settle into a routine, they were often catching stars who had worked main unit the night before or who might have been arriving from a prior commitment. Fowler recalls Peter Facinelli, who plays Dr. Carlisle Cullen, flying in from New York at midnight and sitting in the makeup chair at three a.m.

"You're the first person the talent sees in the morning, so how they leave the trailer is often how the day is going to go for them," Fowler said. "The makeup trailer is where everybody's stories of the night before come up, where people talk about their hopes and dreams and everything. So we made the atmosphere comfortable in the makeup trailers. We bought a coffeemaker, so everyone had a good cup of coffee, which was appreciated. Makeup artists

> THE SECOND UNIT TYPICALLY HANDLES STUNTS AND ACTION, PICKUP SCENES, [AND] SEQUENCES DELEGATED BY THE DIRECTOR.

"I love making people beautiful, and I loved making beautiful vampires. This is not a horror show but, as in the books, a beauty show. These vampires look unearthly beautiful. One thing we do with vampires that you don't do on every makeup is shading, which brings out the bone structure. You start with a base of white, then do a pale color and add the shading to bring out more of a sculptural look, which means using a darker color around the temples, under the cheekbones, the chin, around the eyes a bit."

—JOANN FOWLER, MAKEUP LEAD, SECOND UNIT

Dakota Fanning as Jane.

read the people they're working with. We try to gauge their moods—it's most of our job, really. We're good empaths. We have a very privileged position, because we do get to know the actors, and we all spend a lot of time together for a short period of time."

Just as important as great makeup are believable sets. One of the iconic settings of the books and films is the Cullen house, that mysterious place in the woods that Bella first visited when Edward took her home to meet the "family." On the first film, the production got permission to film at a home in Portland owned by a local executive. It was a three-story house in a forested area, with floor-to-ceiling glass walls and stark white walls. When the production shifted from Portland to Vancouver, a new Cullen house had to be found.

The Twilight Saga: New Moon needed the Cullen house for only one scene, but it was a key one—Bella's birthday party. The house in *New Moon* was a bit of a "cheat," as Bill Bannerman called it, a home in the Vancouver area that was similar in style to the original, with Bella's party set in what was ostensibly another room of the house.

But the Cullen house was a major location in *Eclipse*, including being the site of the big party for the happy graduates of Forks High School. "The Cullen house was such a small component of *New Moon*, but for *Eclipse* it was 'We have to build the whole house!'" said David Slade.

There was precedent to re-creating a Portland location, notably the hundred-year-old house that served as Bella's home in the first film, which had been meticulously re-created for *New Moon*, right down to the stucco finish of Bella's bedroom wall. But to re-create the original Cullen house was ambitious. Bill Bannerman estimated the "footprint" of the three-story Portland house at 7,000 or 8,000 square feet.

"For me, that house was a big character in the first film," production designer Austerberry noted. "For *Eclipse*, we needed a lot of scenes at the Cullen house, and we wanted the feel of a real location and being able to see the outside, so it felt like we were at a real house."

Austerberry recalled discussing the idea of re-creating the Portland location during his *Eclipse* job interview with Wyck Godfrey and David Slade. The producer knew the location from *Twilight* well and also felt strongly they needed to re-create it. What Godfrey wasn't prepared for was *where* Austerberry wanted to build it. "We couldn't go back to Portland, so my initial instinct was to build it outside," Godfrey recalled. "Paul said, 'That will never work. I can build it *inside*.'"

THE CULLEN HOUSE WAS A MAJOR LOCATION IN *Eclipse*.

Two stories of the three-story house rose on a 20,000-square-foot Vancouver soundstage. Austerberry had all the photographs and digital PDF files needed to re-create the Portland house, and he also was granted permission to re-create the look by the architectural firm that had originally designed it. "We not only re-created the house with floor-to-ceiling windows, but the driveway and garage and a fifteen-foot ribbon of forest and vegetation around the home," noted Bill Bannerman.

Bannerman observed that it would have been a shock for anyone who knew that house to seemingly find it in a nondescript, hangar-sized warehouse in south Vancouver. "If you knew that house and were blindfolded and taken to our set, you could look out the windows onto the forest and, for a moment, believe you were in the real house. The greens department in *Eclipse* was probably three times the size of *New Moon* because of those kinds of demands, and they did a brilliant job—beautiful, flawless. We

The re-creation of the Cullen house included the driveway, the garage, and a strip of forest around the perimeter.

Interiors dressed on the set of the Cullen house.

> "In *Eclipse*, we needed to be in several rooms of the Cullen house—most important, the kitchen area, which is pretty unique.... At the outset, [the plan was to] give up the look of that kitchen and move that sequence into another room, but the unanimous reaction was to keep the integrity of the creative vision and storytelling by rebuilding the house [from *Twilight*]."
>
> —BILL BANNERMAN, CO-PRODUCER

did take some license and widened some hallways and raised some ceiling levels to accommodate camera crews and the logistics of filming in tight areas. But that house was re-created up to the second floor and detailed out, right down to decorations and wood tones, counters, fixtures, lighting, and plumbing."

The post-graduation party at the Cullen house put the soundstage set to good use. For the first time, human outsiders other than Bella arrive en masse at the mysterious house in the woods. Aguirresarobe's camera could film the exterior as partygoers arrived and could even follow them inside the house and into rooms not seen since *Twilight*.

The production team kept in touch with Stephenie Meyer to make sure they threw a party faithful to the novel. "In her book, she's very descriptive of the colors with which Alice has decorated the house, the kind of light lining the driveway," Paul Austerberry said. "I slightly deviated but adhered in the design to what was in the book, because it was so detailed. Red permeates the book, and there were red and purple lights, which we did outside and inside, and purple burgundy, which is Bella's favorite color."

The graduation party scenes would be able to feature both the exterior and the interior simultaneously, with the wall-sized windows enabling arriving partygoers to see the festivities going on inside, while guests inside had clear views outside. Because of the windows,

> "IT'S THE MOST IMPRESSIVE SET I'VE EVER
> BEEN INVOLVED IN."
>
> —WYCK GODFREY, PRODUCER

"One of the characters I had fun writing was Bella's classmate Jessica, played by Anna Kendrick. In the book, Stephenie doesn't really describe what went on in the graduation. I felt there had to be a valedictorian speech, and who would be the one to do that? Kendrick is such a great actress—she just *pops* on the screen—so I wrote the speech for her."

—MELISSA ROSENBERG,
SCREENWRITER

Anna Kendrick as Jessica.

"I hadn't read the books until I knew I was going to be auditioning for *Twilight*. There wasn't a script yet, so I read the first couple books to get a feel for the characters and story line—and I fell in love. I knew I had to be a part of this. For those of us who have been in all three films, we've gone through this amazing journey together, and it's united us as a family. It's nice to have that, because at times it can be overwhelming.

"I definitely share qualities with Alice. She's energetic, positive, and is extremely close to her family and motivated by the desire to protect them. These are all things I can relate to. And although it was already there, I've gained more of a sense of confidence and sassiness with Alice's character over the course of the films. We've intensely studied the characters to play them as true to the books as possible. The fans know everything about these characters, and it's important that we live up to their expectations.

"Hair, makeup, and wardrobe is a big part of my transition into the character of Alice. It takes about two hours between the white body makeup, yellow contacts, and pixie wig—the result is very different from how I look in real life. Once we put the contacts in, it puts you in a different place. You lose your peripheral vision, so your interactions are isolated and it really puts you in the role.

"The most physically challenging scenes for me were learning how to pitch a baseball in *Twilight* and the fight sequences in *Eclipse*. It took a lot of professional training and tons of practice to get the moves just right.

"Emotionally, the toughest scene for me was in *New Moon*, when I have to go to Bella and tell her my brother is about to kill himself. Vampires don't cry, and the yellow contacts limit the emotion you can play through your eyes, which is a big part of how I act. It was extremely challenging to work around those limitations."

The stunts took a lot of practice.

An Interview with Kellan Lutz ❧ Emmett Cullen ❧

"I first read the books before we started shooting [*Twilight*], and I really enjoy the series as a fan. I have found that I embody Emmett. Emmett is a fun-loving, happy-go-lucky guy, like I am. Emmett is also a protector and willing to fight to protect what he loves, and I am that protector-type in real life.

"My favorite parts of *Eclipse* were the fight scenes. I convinced the director to let me do a lot of my own stunts, so that was an incredible experience. It was tough, but so much fun. I've found [I have] a true passion for stunts and action, and I hope to translate that through future work.

"Since we've been working in colder climates [throughout the series], I've learned that staying bundled up when off-set is a must, while on set I've learned to always keep my blood pumping by either jogging or doing a few push-ups. Canada can be quite freezing, and if you don't take care of yourself, it's easy to get sick—always take your vitamins, they help!

"From the start, the cast has gotten along. We have spent a great amount of time together while filming the movies and have created a strong bond. It's funny, because I don't feel the success of the films has changed me. I do the same things as normal, although I have been busier and career doors have opened for me. When I'm out and about, I'm sometimes recognized, but I'm always grateful and happy to say 'hi' to the fans.

"My personal process for getting into character is to first do as much research as possible on the character. It was great having Stephenie on set so I could ask her questions about Emmett. I also like to create my own backstory on a character, and I make notes I can refer to. Hair, makeup, and wardrobe are the final touches, and when they're completed, not only are you mentally in character, you can actually look in a mirror and see yourself as that person, so it really helps you completely become that character.

"My definition of acting as an art form is simply me showing you that I can skillfully change your perception of me through language, context, and body language. You can definitely call it a transformation, and it is my passion."

You could not only walk into the Cullen house set, it had a driveway and you could drive a car up, get out, and walk up the front steps. In the graduation party, we could see guests arrive, go inside and walk to the top of the stairs, go into the living room, the kitchen, and the outdoor terrace. It was like a real house, only with walls we could remove. We also made the big glass windows able to swivel two or three degrees within the window frame, just a slight tweaking to angle them, which was enough to hide lights and cameras and reflections."

—PAUL AUSTERBERRY, PRODUCTION DESIGNER

Alice's fancy lighting decorates the Cullen house for the graduation party.

even interior scenes required the special effects department, headed by supervisor Alex Burdett, to operate wind machines to rustle the trees, giving life to the set. It was pure movie magic, the only "cheat" being Edward's bedroom for an important scene between Edward and Bella.

"Edward's bedroom is on the third floor, but there was no room in the soundstage to build a third floor," Austerberry said. "But we really didn't need it. The windows were all the same [in the house and Edward's bedroom], so we cheated, and when we struck the living room set, we re-dressed it to look like Edward's bedroom."

The art and construction departments were "unbelievably efficient and fast" in re-creating the Cullens' house, Bannerman recalled. The set was available earlier than expected and became a plan B option if weather were to interfere with scheduled location work. For

Ashley Greene as Alice Cullen.

the late-summer shooting schedule of *The Twilight Saga: Eclipse*, "bad" weather meant too much sunshine. "Normally, 'weather cover' is when you arrive at an exterior location and it's pouring rain and you have to go inside," Bannerman explained. "On this movie, [we] began filming in August, so there was a little bit more sunshine in Vancouver. Because our vampires had to be under overcast skies, we had to go film some-place out of the sun, and with the luxury of having the Cullen house, that enabled us to use that set as weather cover."

*Edward Cullen's bedroom set
included historical touches.*

"In *New Moon*, I was very much a supporting part. In *Eclipse*, Edward is fighting to be active. But it's not really him that's driving the story. Unseen forces are driving the story. . . . At the same time, Edward is trying to push his way into it."

—ROBERT PATTINSON, ACTOR

Victoria's Vendetta

Bryce Dallas Howard as Victoria.

In both the novels and the films, Victoria is the nightmare that won't go away. In *Twilight*, she appeared with James and Laurent on the mountaintop as Bella watched the Cullens play vampire baseball. The three rogues were nomadic feral vampires who wore the clothing and accessories of their victims. James decided to make Bella his prey, and the chase led to Phoenix, where Bella suffered the vampire's bite. Emmett and Jasper destroyed James, and Edward sucked the vampire venom from Bella's wound, saving her. It was a happy ending that did not sit well with Victoria, who made it her mission to see Edward lose *his* beloved.

"I love writing Victoria. She's such a delicious character, and [it's] so much fun to go into her world," Melissa Rosenberg said. "There is some justification for her actions. She's heart-broken and pissed off at the loss of her mate."

Victoria pursued Bella in *The Twilight Saga: New Moon*, but in *The Twilight Saga: Eclipse* her shadow loomed over the whole story as she collected her force of newborns in Seattle (the resulting rash of homicides, missing persons, and serial-killer fears generated headlines).

With the Cullens protecting Bella, and Alice using her telepathic ability to sense danger coming, the unknown Riley can marshal the army without tracking on Alice's

> "THERE IS SOME JUSTIFICATION FOR HER ACTIONS. SHE'S HEARTBROKEN AND PISSED OFF AT THE LOSS OF HER MATE."

mental radar. When the plot is finally discovered, the Cullens and the wolves put aside their differences and join forces to protect Bella and to fight the newborns.

"Victoria . . . brings in her army of newborns, which is a whole new cast of characters," noted line producer Bill Bannerman. "That meant more action, more dynamics, and more needs in not only hair, wardrobe, and makeup but stunts and action as well."

The casting of Victoria in *The Twilight Saga: Eclipse* marked a shake-up in the ensemble. The original Victoria, the sultry Rachelle Lefevre, was replaced by actress Bryce Dallas Howard. Lefevre, who had portrayed the character in *Twilight* and *The Twilight Saga: New Moon*, did not continue in the role due to scheduling conflicts with another commitment the actress had made.

Stephenie Meyer had originally envisioned Bryce Dallas Howard in the role of Victoria for the first film, but the actress had just given birth when *Twilight* was being cast, so the timing didn't work out. Howard was thrilled at the chance to step into the role that got away.

"I was definitely obsessed with *Twilight*; I saw it on opening day," said Howard. "I actually became quite fanatical about Edward—he's just so dangerous, he could kill Bella at any moment! It's all enthralling and exciting and very romantic. So I completely understand the fascination with the books and the franchise."

"Bryce Dallas Howard is the most stunningly beautiful vampire you'll see. The only reason we put makeup on her is to cover freckles. She's so naturally pale that the makeup looks like velvet, and we just added a very simple eyeline to her makeup. She made a beautiful, beautiful vampire."

—JOANN FOWLER, MAKEUP LEAD, SECOND UNIT

An Interview with Bryce Dallas Howard ❧ Victoria ❧

"I already loved the books and the movies [before being cast in *Eclipse*]. I am what could be called a 'Twi-Hard.' After I saw *Twilight* for the fifth time, I actually had a friend make me Post-it notes with Rob's face that said 'Live dangerously.' But it was very intimidating to step into a role created by another actor. When it was announced that I would be playing Victoria in *Eclipse*, there was a huge outcry of support for Rachelle. I personally feel that was totally justified, because she depicted Victoria with complete devotion in two memorable performances. I just wanted to both honor Stephenie's creation and live up to Rachelle's beautiful portrayal of the character.

"It was also a bit intimidating because everyone on the films has been through a lot together and formed true, lasting friendships. I didn't want to come in and assume I would be included—but that is exactly what happened. The cast and crew were so welcoming; everyone wanted to make the best film possible. My life has changed in that I now have some new and very dear friends whom I never would have met had it not been for this film. I just adore that cast.

"Rereading the books helped me enormously. Stephenie has created a world that just sucks you in. It was very intense, and quite a mind trip, to play a vampire, a character who was once human

but is no longer . . . . David Slade really understood the vampire psychology, and we had innumerable conversations exploring how to tap into that mindset and portray it on-screen.

"If you yourself don't believe in the circumstances or the world, neither will the audience. The audience has invested their money and time in having you take them on a journey, and the only way to do that is to experience the ride yourself. I do that by research, daydreaming, talking to myself in front of a mirror, getting in a room with the other actors and trying it all out, relying on the filmmakers and actors, and trusting the words you've been given to ultimately carry you. The hair, makeup, and costume also informs a lot and is itself a challenging and exciting process where, I always find, the character is discovered and comes to life.

"I think what we were hoping for in *Eclipse* was to dramatize Bella's struggle—she is literally choosing between life and death. For that reason, the stakes have to feel that much higher. I believe that David struck a remarkable balance in the film of spectacle and intimacy.

"Definitely, the most intense scene for me was at the end of the film—the mountaintop. The fight with Edward was pretty fantastic. We trained for quite a while, but when you get there on the day and you are surrounded by the set and your emotion is going and they yell 'Action' and you are flying around and trees are falling—it's pretty exciting and feels pretty darn real!

"On location, the elements are always a factor. Sometimes, it was like, 'I did my best given I only had one take because there was a snowstorm coming and it was ten below zero and I was acting to a tennis ball.' Of course, there are those magical moments when the elements are really on your side—the wind blows at the perfect moment, or the temperature informs your emotional state. I live for when that happens: when nature and storytelling align."

"Someone like Victoria is just listening to [her] instincts. In the human world, everyone gets caught up with morality and what's right and wrong. That's what is so fascinating to the Volturi about the Cullens: that they're not listening to their instincts but are caught up in human notions of what's right and wrong."

—BRYCE DALLAS HOWARD, ACTRESS

"The nature of vampires is they are far gone from their humanity, and they're bored. In Victoria's pursuit of Bella, there's also that aspect of her drawing up something interesting for her to do, playing with her food a little bit."

—MELISSA ROSENBERG, SCREENWRITER

Young student Riley before he is transformed.

The character of Riley was presented in two incarnations: The first was just a brief glimpse of the young college student, and the second was in full vampire mode. On the costume side, the difference was that the student Riley wore jeans and a casual earth-toned jacket, while the vampire Riley was more "hipster-looking," costume designer Tish Monaghan said, with a darker color palette and dark skinny-leg jeans, boots, and a button-up shirt.

"In the first sequences where we meet Riley, there is a rain that falls like a phosphorescent waterfall—an oneiric and premonitory image that changes the life of this character," said Aguirresarobe. "Victoria and Riley's world is the opposite of the world of Bella, Edward, and Jacob. Victoria and Riley move within a more sinister space. Colder. An example of the light and contrasts that surround these characters is a sequence under a bridge where Victoria tries to get Riley to love her. It's in the night, in the shadows, and that's where they move freely."

The rain was provided courtesy of supervisor Alex Burdett's special effects team. The work required his crew, usually consisting of about twenty-five members, to swell to forty. The team rained out an entire block and two back alleys of downtown Vancouver for scenes of Riley running in the rain. They then moved to a dock in south Vancouver, where he becomes Victoria's victim.

"We had a crane and about twenty rain towers down on the dock, with five water trucks," Burdett explained. "The next night we had two one-hundred-ten-ton cranes with a rain truss and another twenty rain towers for the downtown Vancouver work. A truss is basically a fancy sprinkler head that disperses water in a pattern. The art director wanted very

Vampire Riley takes a tour of the Swan house.

"Victoria and
Riley move within
a more sinister
space. Colder."

"Victoria is driven by one of the great drives in theatrical tradition: revenge. Actually, the most complex rehearsals, where we made the most notes, were with Bryce and Xavier Samuel, who plays Riley. We rehearsed and rehearsed because of the complexity of what the character is doing. Is Victoria playing Riley? Maybe, but maybe not. That will be up to everyone to decide. I don't think it's as simple as saying she is manipulating him, although she is an expert evader and manipulator. I would like to think she has priorities. Maybe she does love Riley on some level, but when it comes down to it, revenge is driving her, and at a certain point she will jettison everything and go after that."

—DAVID SLADE, DIRECTOR

Performing stunts in the rain provided by the special effects team.

large water drops, which is why we had so many water trucks and so many rain towers, because the bigger the drops, the less area our tower will cover. The water towers were twenty feet tall and mounted on five-story buildings. The rain trusses are eighty feet long, with four-foot-diameter pipe with clusters of rain heads that we'd pick up with a hundred-ton construction crane and aim over everything, moving it around to get full coverage."

For stunt coordinator John Stoneham Jr., whose recent work included the disaster epic *2012*, the new film was a huge rigging show. The actors and stunt performers playing vampires were put in harnesses with pick points connecting with thin wires rigged to systems that flew them as if they were making mighty vampire leaps. "David wanted them to look as heavy and real as possible, not floaty like in a fairy tale," Stoneham noted. "And when they hit the ground, it's going to be hard. We had air movers, little cylinders under the surface, so when they touched down, it would blow out air and give the realistic effect of dirt kicking up as they land. It was all about realism."

The stunts and wirework ranged from an early sequence in which the Cullens and the wolves chase Victoria, to the final battle scenes. The stunt coordinator noted that this included a new wrinkle in the established look of vampire speed that fit into the director's desire for realism. "David wanted to capture everything in-camera if he could, so the impetus was on unobtrusive, photo-realistic effects," said visual effects coordinator Jeremy Ball. "The sequence where wolves and vampires chase Victoria through the woods will, I think, have a lot of people scratching their heads as to how it was achieved. David really set the bar high by developing a practical technique for having actors run through the forest."

It began with the mechanical effects of Alex Burdett's unit and was digitally enhanced by Image Engine. "David Slade didn't like the high-speed running which was achieved by over-cranking the camera to make things look fast—you just notice it, that's 'bionic man' technology," said Alex Burdett, referring to the 1970s TV show *The Six Million Dollar Man*. "So we experimented with putting actors on carriages and towing them while they ran [in place] and a camera car filmed them."

Burdett's special effects team developed two approaches: one for wide-open spaces, another for

Kellan Lutz shows off his "pick points" (left) for wirework stunts, and the rig (lower right) that gives his running superspeed.

closed-in spaces, such as the opening forest chase scene. "One we called the 'magic carpet,' which was a large piece of conveyor belt, eighty to one hundred ten feet long and six feet wide, which the actors ran on while a truck dragged the belt at fifty kilometers [thirty-one miles per hour]—which, with them running, had a real-time look as if they were moving at seventy kilometers [forty-four miles per hour]," Burdett explained.

"The other method was a high-speed quad—basically a souped-up golf cart that could pull a treadmill on forest trails and places too narrow for a truck. We secured the performer to the treadmill. Every time you see a vampire running, it's one of those techniques, and we used them more times than I could count. A lot of it was for the final battle with the newborns, although because of the space restrictions, we used high-speed winches to pull the conveyor."

The "vamp-timing," as Image Engine referred to the speed effects, then added details and augmented the real-time physical effects. "We'd take the practical elements and add details like dust being kicked up," said Robin Hackl, sequence supervisor and on-set plate supervisor. "It got complicated, because they filmed the actors on set at a higher frame rate, so we'd add our process of sweetening and retiming that. We also picked key moments, like someone swinging their fist, and exaggerated the speed."

For the Victoria chase sequence, the special effects supervisor and a six-person crew worked with the director and the director of photography to rig lightweight and radio-controllable cameras in a forest in North Vancouver. After start and stop points were nailed down and all was cleared with the production's location department and a film liaison from the Vancouver parks board, the camera-and-wire setup was rigged. "We'd use two base trees as our start and end points, and also as tieback trees for safety, because we put quite a bit of pressure on the wire," Burdett explained. "We built a cable line and a carriage upon which the camera was mounted to ride on the cable."

"For the chase scene, we had a stunt performer for Victoria jumping across a ravine that was eighty to ninety feet wide. We had a high line from one side to the other, and a ratchet and a descender to yank her across. A lot of the rigging depended on the environment. We had big jumps, and leaping from tree to tree. Each location was different. A good rigger is a problem solver— they'll come up with the best ideas for how to rig what's needed to safely do the shot."

—JOHN STONEHAM JR., STUNT COORDINATOR

Riley, like all vampires in Meyer's mythology, could go about his grim business under overcast skies but, as Aguirresarobe observed, "it's in the night, in the shadows" where Riley and Victoria move freely. That meant the kind of victims who would frequent bars, nightclubs, and other venues for the nightlife. "It was anyone who might be out and about [on] a Seattle street between ten in the evening and two in the morning," Monaghan said. "It was a cross section of university students, hipsters, and musicians, a businessman who had gone straight from the office to a bar."

The production had a core group of twenty-one newborns, who, given the action required, were played by stunt performers. Their wardrobe was off the rack, with multiples of six or seven for each of them. Their occupation dictated their costumes; for example, a slacker rock-and-roller was dressed differently from a young business executive out for an evening.

What all the newborns' costumes had in common, however, was that Monaghan's department chose warmer colors than the typically cooler tones worn by the Cullens.

"I didn't want the newborns to stand out too much, to be an onslaught on the senses and steal a lot of focus," Monaghan explained. "We took the clothing for the newborns and trashed them, aged them. That was a very methodical approach for a four- or five-person department headed by Lily Yuen, who was our head breakdown artist. They thought about where the wear marks would be; they created a backstory for the characters.

"For example, even though it's only a couple weeks of story time, they don't sleep. You have to imagine where the newborns would be at night. Maybe they're hiding out or running through a forest, so their pants are getting caught; their footwear gets worn out. Then the costumes were sanded and overdyed to reflect that. Lily took a very scientific approach."

"The newborns are regular vampires, just less in control. They have very short attention spans, they're less controllable and more violent, they don't think before they act. They're running at a higher heart rate, if you will. That creates a dangerous creature. This contrasts to the Cullens and the Volturi, who are never out of control."

—WYCK GODFREY, PRODUCER

Riley and the newborns.

"The newborns are not zombies; they're not monsters. They are essentially people who have no control when they smell blood. You don't want to get into simplification, so we kept it as subtle and naturalistic as possible."

—DAVID SLADE, DIRECTOR

"Before the newborns came out of the water, [the makeup team] had to be out in the water, up to our waists, touching up the makeup that would keep breaking down in water—they couldn't come out with pink skin! One of the funny things was the stunt-man we dubbed 'the Big Ball of Death.' His head was really big, and with all the white makeup on, your eyes kept going to him, and not where [they were] supposed to go. We had to keep moving 'the Big Ball of Death' to the back!"

—JOANN FOWLER, MAKEUP LEAD, SECOND UNIT

Since so many of the scenes with the newborns were shot in second unit, JoAnn Fowler took the lead in their makeup. "We didn't want them to look too much different from the Cullens," Fowler explained. "They were all stunt people, because the newborns had to do a lot of training and fighting. But vampires don't bleed or bruise. The challenge of a vampire film is keeping them pale and making the makeup look like skin, particularly when performers are in scenes where they're fighting, sweating, and getting thrown down and dirty."

For the second-unit makeup team, each day started in the trailers, with newborns, stunt doubles, and main actors getting made up either in the main seven-seat trailer or in three additional trailers with three makeup chairs each. Fowler would oversee and make sure the work was being completed. Then more than a dozen makeup artists were off to the set for the constant retouching the vampires required.

"It was a fairly easy makeup," Fowler noted. "The hard part was to keep them looking good all day. You had to add makeup to places where you don't usually apply makeup—hands, neck, the inside of the ears. We actually airbrushed the back of the ear with a thick, inky color, because light from the back makes the ear translucent and it looks red. Makeup will come off hands in, like, two seconds. So you had to be constantly touching up an actor's makeup; you couldn't stop, and you had to cover every centimeter of skin.

"We'd go in between shots to do touch-ups. The production understood the challenges, and if somebody needed a touch-up [before the cameras rolled], I'd go to the first AD [assistant director] and they'd stop, no questions asked. We didn't abuse the privilege, but we had to keep a really sharp eye."

Two key players: Bree (above left, at center) and Riley (right).

"We all loved *Eclipse* because it's the one with the most action and the most male appeal. But, that said, it's still all about Bella. The newborn army represents her fear of what her future might look like once she becomes a vampire. It's weighing on her mind."

—WYCK GODFREY, PRODUCER

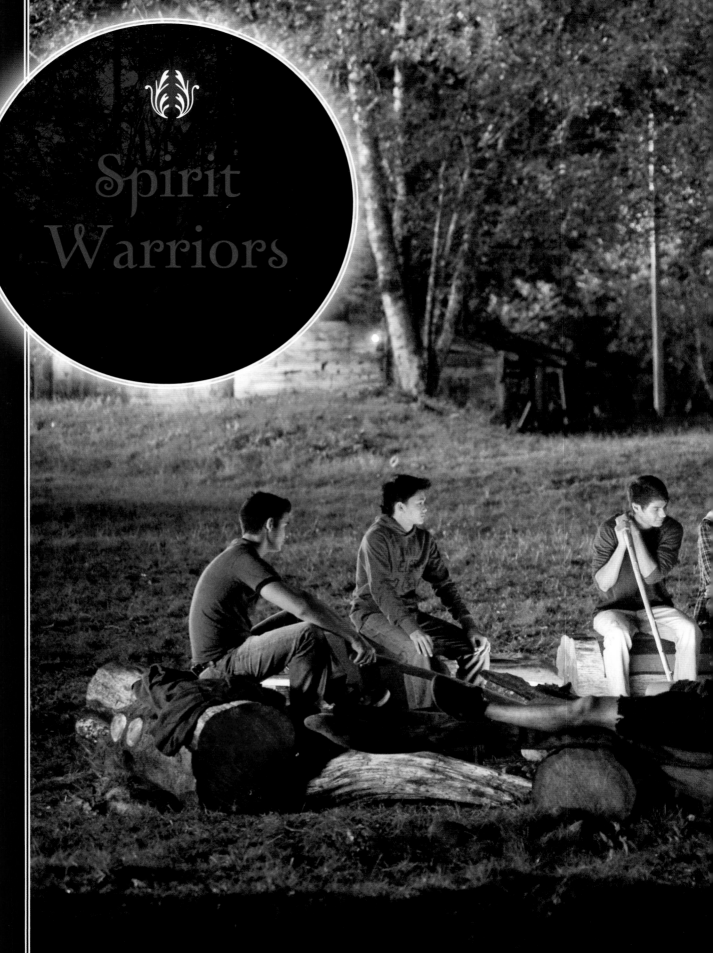

Spirit
Warriors

Bella and Jacob join the Quileute bonfire to hear the tribe's legends.

In ECLIPSE, Bella looked into the crackling bonfire. She felt comfortable sitting in the circle with her Quileute friends, waiting to have the privilege of hearing their legends. "I was treated like someone who belonged," she would recall.[4]

Stephenie Meyer set the stage for Bella to hear a story that would speak to her decision to become a vampire. And as it had been done since prehistory, the gathering around the fire told the story of the people. It was a history they wanted to share with Bella, a story of vampires and werewolves.

The Twilgiht Saga: Eclipse screenplay picks up the ancient tale in 1750 when two Quileute warriors encountered what seemed to be a Spaniard standing over the bodies of two dead girls from the tribe. The stranger was a vampire,

THE THIRD WIFE'S SACRIFICE SAVED THE TRIBE.

and the warriors phased into wolves. The wolves' teeth tore the Spaniard apart, but not before the vampire killed one of them. It took fire to finish off the Cold One. The Quileute villagers lived in fear that more vampires would come.

Their fears were realized the day a vampiress in Spanish dress appeared, hungry for revenge at the death of her mate. She was wreaking havoc, and Taha Aki, the tribe's chief, was the only "spirit warrior" left alive to phase into a wolf and fight back. The chief's third wife, who had no magical powers, watched helplessly as the vampiress gained the upper

The mysterious Spanish vampire attacks Quileute villagers.

Bella (Stewart) shares a moment with Jacob (Lautner).

hand. But the third wife had courage. She pulled out a dagger—and plunged it into her heart. The smell of blood distracted the vampiress, enabling the chief wolf to destroy her. The third wife's sacrifice saved the tribe.

In researching how to re-create the old Quileute village, the production ran into a bitter truth of the past. In the late nineteenth century, an arsonist torched the village, and the flames consumed much of the history of the people. "Their longhouses were burned down; they lost all their artifacts," Paul Austerberry noted. "It's a sad story. So they didn't have as much history as the other bands in the region. There was no photographic reference for that nation, either, so we had to re-create a similar village. We were concerned that we not upset the Quileute Nation, because we had to look at various nations of the Olympic Peninsula. I

had to take pieces of other groups; it became an amalgamation. The goal was making it feel like you were in the right world."

The Quileute village was built in an inlet north of Vancouver and south of the little town of Squamish. "Paul Austerberry's research found that indigenous tribes in this region basically built their villages to be mobile," Bill Bannerman explained. "Depending on the season of the year, they could tear apart their structures, put them in canoes or portage, and move them. The structures in our village reflected this authenticity."

The location had some disadvantages. It wasn't big enough to accommodate more than a few longhouses, and the director of photography had to work around less-than-ideal sun conditions. "Often, the DP will want a little rim light or backlight, with angles looking toward the sun, not into it. Unfortunately, the bay had a mountainside that blocked the sun most of the day,"

Austerberry said. "We had about a one-and-a-half-hour window when the sun was right for the wide-angle shots. Poor Javier had to deal with that the next day [when shots went tighter]. He had to block off massive amounts of direct sun for the front, when we'd rather have had it from behind. Production design has to work hand in hand with the DP, and when you're going to be outside, you always have to consider the sun. In this case, there wasn't much choice—it was dictated by the bay and the location."

The set came together with construction, props, and set dressing. Wooden racks were lashed together for drying fish, tobacco, and skunkweed; three big longhouses were squeezed into the inlet; a smokehouse on stilts was built on the beach;

A lot of historical research went into the design of the Quileute village.

74

and the set was dressed with artifacts. Four period canoes were also re-created for the scene of the invading vampiress, with frightened villagers jumping in and shoving off. "The real canoes are built out of cedar logs, but we built ours of solid Styrofoam we cut with chainsaws to look like it had been hewn out of wood," Austerberry said with a smile. "But they worked, they floated!"

Tish Monaghan had to design costumes faithful to what the Quileutes of the time might have worn. It led, she said, to "the most interesting bit of research," including poring over online sources for diary accounts, logs, and descriptions from explorers and seamen who encountered the tribes of the Pacific Northwest coastline. She researched books in brick-and-mortar libraries, referred to Edward Curtis's period photographs, and looked at the works of period painters. But a breakthrough came during several museum visits to Simon Fraser University and its Museum of Archaeology and Ethnology, and to the Museum of Anthropology at the University of British Columbia. "From northern British Columbia to southern Washington, and even into Oregon, there was a similarity to the clothing—cedar bark," Monaghan explained. "Both museums had original artifacts from the seventeen

"THEY WORE CEDAR CAPES AND CEDAR WRAPS THAT WENT AROUND THE BODY AND WERE HELD TOGETHER WITH BONE OR TWINE."

"Photographically, the Quileute village sequence was treated in a different, peculiar way. It was filmed in warm tones with slight contrasts. I tried, within a realistic tone, to transpose our imaginations back to what could have happened three hundred years ago. The sequence has a certain documentary feel that is used to enhance the tragedy of what happens within the tribe, without relinquishing the aesthetic aspects of the film itself."

—JAVIER AGUIRRESAROBE, DIRECTOR OF PHOTOGRAPHY

hundreds and burial sites, with examples of the cedar work clothing. Although they were in disrepair, I was able to study them up close, and [the museum] allowed me to take photographs.

"It was woven cedar bark, taken from the trees," she explained. "They harvested the bark at a certain time of year, tore the bark into strips, soaked them in water to make them soft and malleable, and then [wove them]. They wore cedar capes and cedar wraps that went around the body and were held together with bone or twine. There was a certain amount of modesty. The women had wraps over their shoulders. The men tended to wear the skirt wraps and usually nothing for their feet, although we gave our performers something for their feet." In the rain, the cedar bark would swell and protect the wearer, like a poncho.

Monaghan discovered that modern-day indigenous people made traditional cedar bark clothing for museum installation and public sale. She found a cedar bark cape in Whistler, but a $25,000 price tag was prohibitive for a department that had to outfit some seventy-five Quileute villagers. In the end, the cedar bark clothing was simulated by "burlap erosion cloth," a ground cover used by landscapers. "The set decoration department had some, and it looked fantastic," Monaghan noted. "We got about one hundred feet for a hundred dollars! We also used rugs and loosely woven hemp."

The village chief and the chief's wife got special attention. "I wanted to set them apart," Monaghan said. "I used a raw silk for the wife's costume; it looked like a simple

woven blanket. That was inspired by some of the research I did at the two museums. I also added decorative red wool, which was woven into the borders and is reminiscent of traditional point blankets. The bulk of the tribe was dressed in the naturally colored replicas of cedar bark clothing, which is brownish and earth-toned, while the chief and his wife were in neutral, off-white tones."

Although Tippett Studio created the modern-day wolves, Image Engine was given the assignment of creating the "ancient wolves" for the Quileute legend flashback. The computer-generated wolves had to follow the wolf look Tippett Studio established in *The Twilight Saga: New Moon*. "We gave Image Engine our base model to help us all be in the same ballpark," Tippett animation supervisor Tom Gibbons noted.

But there were opportunities for Image Engine to take creative liberties. "There was a little bit of a difference, as we're going back hundreds of years," said Jon Cowley, Image Engine visual effects supervisor. "Our in-house concept team came up with some different looks that we ran by the director and the on-set visual effects supervisor on the production side. It was subtle, but there was the idea that the wolves have evolved over time. Our historical wolves were scraggly, leaner and meaner, and not as well fed as the current-day wolves, who are a little heavier.

"At Image Engine, our character animation is story-driven," Cowley added. "When you work on a film, certain buzzwords pop up that you use to describe the character to your animators. Since the direction on our wolves was that they be photo-realistic, the buzzword was *weight*. Even when the wolves weren't in the frame with something that could give it scale, we wanted them to look big and massive and also very fast. We wanted to sell that balance."

On a wall of his studio office in Berkeley, California, Phil Tippett has a picture that represents a composite of photographs of himself and Ray Harryhausen, the master of stop-motion animation, the traditional art of manipulating a puppet or other articulated object frame by frame to give the illusion of life when filmed. The photo is an example of what Tippett calls the "haunting effect," or the idea of an image that speaks to the viewer, even on an unconscious level. Harryhausen created stop-motion magic for such classic fantasy adventure films as *The 7th Voyage of Sinbad* and *Jason and the Argonauts*.

Tippett represented the next generation, having worked on *Star Wars* and later heading up the creature shop at Industrial Light & Magic before starting his own company, which specialized in stop-motion animation. But so-called "traditional effects" would give way to computer graphics. "When [CG] came in, it was horrible!" Tippett recalled. "The computer was just a box; it was something an accountant worked with! It was very counterintuitive for a craftsperson, for stop-motion animators, to use that. It was a shock, but it was 'go with the flow

"THERE WAS THE IDEA THAT THE WOLVES HAVE EVOLVED OVER TIME."

or get out of the racket.' No one was interested in you if you weren't doing computer graphics. But when I saw *Jurassic Park*, I realized that was the way things were going to be done from now on, so figure it out. Nowadays, I love working with people who know the [digital] tools, while I work with the director, the writer, production designer, and director of photography to get the shot."

For *New Moon*, Tippett Studio had begun with an intense research period, which included visiting a wolf sanctuary outside Los Angeles, California, to study real wolves up close. The "wolf build" ranged from creating a realistic muscle system for the main "hero" model to building a surface mesh that would lay out the "guide splines" to enable the studio's in-house software to automatically interpolate hairs. The color and groom of the fur was developed and detailed.

When the wolves reached the rendering stage and the final image was produced, there were an estimated four million individual hairs per wolf, twice as many hairs as on any other model Tippett Studio had ever created.

In *Eclipse*, the increased vampire activity in the Olympic Peninsula triggers three new wolves to come into being. In addition to the wolf pack already introduced in *New Moon*, Tippett Studio had to create wolves for Quil, Seth, and Leah, the first female wolf. They also had to tailor the wolves to the vision of the new director. "The wolves had been established in the earlier film, so there were certain things you're not going to

Seth

Quil

Leah

Jacob

Paul

Sam

Embry

Jared

Wolf images courtesy Tippett Studio

Wolf stand-ins on set.

"My approach was to go into this world and say, 'I believe that. That could happen!' The wolves were the heroic stars of the second film, but in this one they're now part of the landscape, as real as the trees, the houses, and everything. So my first goal for the wolves was photo-realism. I remember sitting down with Phil [Tippett], either before he had started on *New Moon* or before his shots were finished, and I said, 'Phil, I'm terrified of these wolves.' And he said, 'You know what? So am I!' We both knew that to be heroic enough to stand up to the characters in *New Moon*, they had to look real. In *Eclipse*, it was a point-of-view issue, not [technical] upgrade. Of course, if you are looking at a twelve-foot wolf, it will fill you with awe. But in this movie, it was less about how awesome they were. Now they had to be part and parcel of this world, because there are a lot of things that will fill you with awe and dread and other emotions."

—DAVID SLADE, DIRECTOR

change," said visual effects coordinator Jeremy Ball. "On the other hand, if a filmmaker wants to push a film in a specific direction, there are going to be some parameters that need to be modified—some so slight the average viewer won't even consciously notice."

While most of the team members who created the CG werewolves on *New Moon* were back for *Eclipse*, Eric Leven, Tippett Studio's visual effects supervisor for the production, was "the new kid on the block," as he put it. "I felt so behind, because everyone here had been working on the werewolves for months. I also had to get familiar with the *Twilight* characters. I had to know them so I could make sure they would always be in character."

Tippett Studio had designed the wolves of *The Twilight Saga: New Moon* to match the aesthetic of director Chris Weitz, and they had to shift gears for the photo-realistic approach that director David Slade asked for, Leven recalled. "Our director was very clear about taking this film in a new direction, to make it all about realism," Leven said. "The first film was sort of a fairy tale, the second was very romantic, but this was the first film in which vampires and werewolves really fight."

The months that stretched from autumn into winter were spent trying to crack the new realism. The director brought in specific requests, such as wanting to see the wolves bare their front teeth and gums. "As opposed to a growl, there's something very primal and lizard

brain about seeing a canine creature bare [its] teeth like that—we know to retreat!" Gibbons laughed. "It's much more menacing. David came to this show with a lot of those specific details."

"One of the things David wanted to change was the wolf behavior," Leven recalled. "Chris Weitz had wanted us to push the humanity of the wolves. For example, we used Taylor Lautner's eyes for the eyes of the Jacob wolf. David wanted us to push the wolf-ness of the wolves, that these are animals. Also, instead of using paws as hands, we went back to the fact that wolves essentially use their mouth more like hands, and their front paws for balance. So in the big battle scene, they don't paw at the newborns; they go after them with their jaws and use their paws for balance."

By December, the visual effects studio thought it had shots that reflected what the director desired. The Tippett team traveled from their studio to Southern California to meet with Slade and show him a scene of Bella and the Jacob wolf. But Slade wanted to push it even further. "He said, 'I'm not seeing the fine resolution of hairs I'm expecting to see,'" Leven recalled. "David didn't want to see the clumping of hairs around the belly. He wanted scraggly hairs."

The problem was that each wolf had some four million individual hairs, and crunching the numbers to create a high-resolution computer-generated figure would be hugely expensive. Essentially, from *New Moon* to *Eclipse*, Tippett Studio would triple its hair renders. "One of those

> "DAVID WANTED US TO PUSH THE WOLF-NESS OF THE WOLVES, THAT THESE ARE ANIMALS."

The detail of the complex fur created for the wolves.

Months were spent perfecting the millions of hairs that made up the fur coat of each computer-generated wolf.

Wolf images courtesy Image Engine

dark secrets is that computers can do anything—if you have an unlimited budget," Tom Gibbons said. "But when you're working on a budget, you do have to be clever. We actually fooled the machine into rendering what we needed."

The solution was to take the "base groom" fur and then, when the wolf model was taken to the final rendering, add a second groom "procedurally"—the CG process by which the computer automatically generates something (in this case, hairs). "What we did was something we'd never done with our fur tool," Leven explained. "What usually happens when you're 'growing' fur is to have it automatically interpolate between key guide splines. But on top of that,

we added millions of extra hairs to interpolate between the hairs that were already interpolating between the guide splines. It was a second layer of procedurally generated hair that had its own groom and styling. This way we got each wolf up to something like eight million hairs."

In January, the Tippett team flew to Southern California and visited the director again, bringing along final high-resolution renders of all the wolves—and this time the director approved. It had been a long creative journey, from the end of summer to the fruitful meeting on January 12, 2010, when the final look was officially nailed down. "It was really about the grooming and clumping of hairs," Leven concluded.

"Quil was straightforward. Seth was different—he's the youngest wolf and kind of the kid brother who looks up to Jacob. He's eager to be part of the gang. Seth doesn't have the size of Sam or Paul. His legs are thinner, and he tends more toward the markings and physique of a coyote. He's more scrappy and comes into his own at the end, because he has a one-on-one fight with Riley. For Leah, we experimented with a slight reshaping of the muzzle, making it longer and thinner, to give the wolf more feminine lines."

—ERIC LEVEN, VISUAL EFFECTS
SUPERVISOR, TIPPETT STUDIO

Quil

Leah

Seth

"My character's lineage is the direct lineage of spirit warriors and shape-shifters. So when the transformations happen, our young men are now carrying the burden and responsibility their forefathers endured to protect the tribe. And the vampires are doing the same thing. It's a clan thing, you know, a challenge to try to be in their higher selves."

—GIL BIRMINGHAM, ACTOR

Chaske Spencer as Sam Uley, Gil Birmingham as Billy Black, and Tinsel Korey as Emily.

"The night we shot the campfire scene was one of the most brutal weather nights. We filmed through the night and into the morning, and it was pounding rain. We had, like, two three-hour time periods when we were just waiting in a tent for the rain to stop. It would stop for fifteen minutes and we'd run out, do the shot quick,

"The campfire scene is important, and not just for expositional purposes—Jacob is letting Bella into his family. My favorite thing about this scene is how comfortable Jacob is with Bella. And then she hears a story that's been passed down from generation to generation. She's the first outsider to hear this story, which is a big deal for her."

—KRISTEN STEWART, ACTRESS

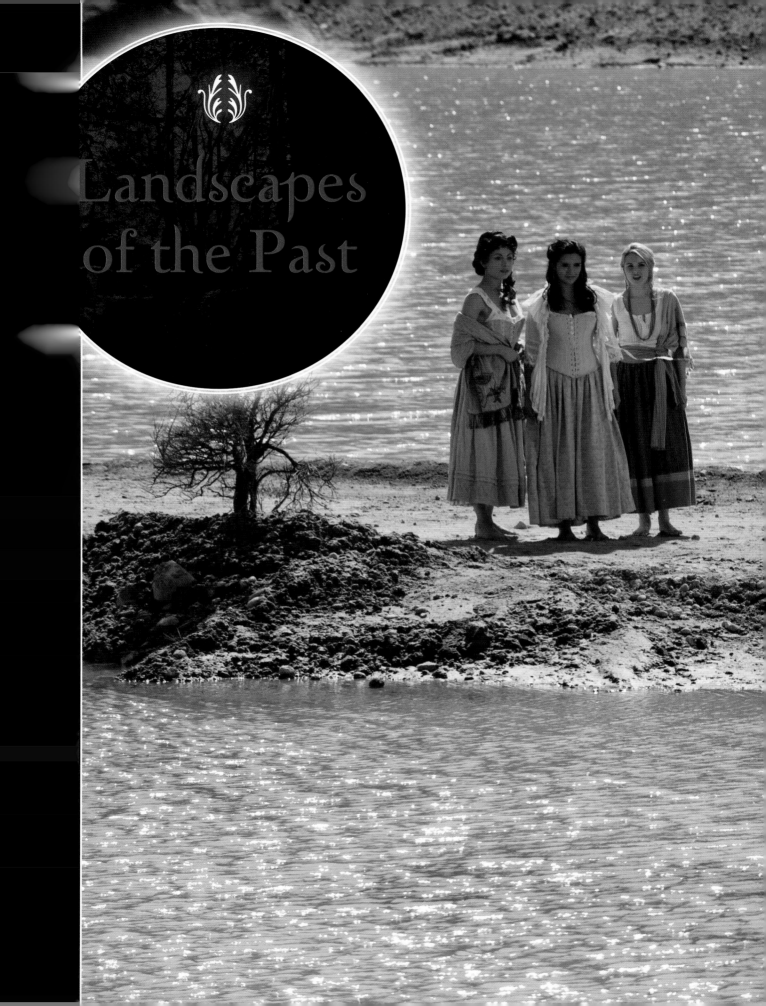

Landscapes
of the Past

Jasper rides out to meet his future.

EXT. DESERT OUTSIDE HOUSTON, TEXAS—NIGHT (1863)

MATCH CUT—JASPER'S HUMAN FACE, tan and flushed with the exertion of riding his horse full throttle down the dirt road. He looks dashing in his Confederate uniform.

> JASPER (V.O.)
> I was riding back to Galveston
> after evacuating a column of women
> and children...when I saw them....

He slows when he sees THREE WOMEN in frayed dresses and bare feet. Their beauty overwhelms him. MARIA, Mexican, black-haired, porcelain-skinned, is flanked by two blonds, LUCY and NETTIE. He dismounts, politely bows. Maria scrutinizes him....

So begins Jasper's vampire origin story, as told in Melissa Rosenberg's screenplay. It's a painful memory he shares with Bella as they compare vampire scars. He recalls how Maria, the vampire who changed him, used him to train her army of newborns. He had been the youngest major of the Texas cavalry, but all his Confederate army training was useless against the freshly changed vampires. Still, he proudly proclaims in the screenplay, "I never lost a fight."

As Jasper related his experiences, it became a cautionary tale of consequences for Bella: If she changed, she would experience the violent bloodlust of all newborns. And then, when she learned Rosalie's story, she also had to consider the cost of losing her humanity.

In the film, Jasper's story is told as the Cullens prepare to battle the newborns. It required three different locations to realize Jasper's story, which moved from his encounter with the vampire sirens to, decades later, his time training newborns for Maria's army. For the training scenes, which Rosenberg's screenplay noted were set in the late nineteenth century, the production team found a barn from the 1890s. "I picked this particular barn because of its interior," Paul Austerberry observed. It had these broad gaps . . . through which wind blew to keep the hay dry, and you got beautiful shafts of sunlight."

"I never choose between stylism and realism—it's all realism to me," David Slade said. "I think shooting in black and white, for instance, when you go to the past is leading the audience, and they're more sophisticated than that. In the stories of Jasper and Rosalie, we are showing vampires when they were in their human form—nobody has ever seen that before! When you consider how well received these films are, how many people will see them, that's a huge responsibility. So I wanted to show what Jasper looked like, what his skin was like, and I couldn't show that in black and white.

"This entire film is really about the consequences of Bella's choice, and the flashbacks in this movie underline that. The

"THIS ENTIRE FILM IS REALLY ABOUT THE CONSEQUENCES OF BELLA'S CHOICE."

flashbacks are all individual, character-driven histories that underline that larger picture. They're not separate but part of the story, and we had to make them as realistic-looking as possible. You will learn the humanity they had and what they lost. Jasper's story alone wanted its own film. These landscapes of the past are quite epic; you have a Western period and a nineteen thirties period. But they are all warnings for Bella."

The image of Jasper riding across the desert wilderness was a chance not only to see his human face but also to evoke mythic Western imagery. "The atmosphere, even though it is night, is warm and enigmatic due to the 'day for night' shoot," said the DP, Aguirresarobe.

Jasper (Rathbone) tells Bella (Stewart) about his past.

"David Slade was adamant that as Jasper rides in, we needed open vistas. Having more information in the frame sells the textures of the environment and makes it work. You don't want to compromise those very specific elements or moments when you need to be able to feel your environment. We could easily have had our Jasper character on a horse and put him on any old dirt road with pine trees and shot him very tight. But when you put him in open valley, it throws the viewer into a completely believable environment that sells the story."

—BILL BANNERMAN, CO-PRODUCER

Principal photography for the film began in a rock quarry to tell Jasper's origin story.

"The contrasts of dust and violence bring to mind scenes from American Western films. The photographic process of Jasper's story was designed to draw us closer to that recurring mythical world of American movies [in which] brutal scenes are combined with romantic gesture."

The costume department researched the Civil War period, guided by the description of Jasper as a Confederate soldier and major in the Texas cavalry. All the costumes, including the bedraggled dresses of sirens and newborns, were made from scratch. For Jackson's uniform and all other Civil War costumes, Tish Monaghan's department contacted three companies specializing in authentic costumes for the many Civil War reenactment societies.

They selected the vendor whose uniforms, they judged, had the nicest wool and the best shape.

Jasper's uniform was composed of a double-breasted jacket, a white linen shirt, a wool vest, wool pants with a yellow stripe, knee-high black boots, gauntlet gloves that went up to his elbows, and the wide-brimmed hat of a Confederate soldier. "There's a lot of pictorial reference for the Civil War, and museum reference of original outfits, paintings, and early photographs," Monaghan noted. "Jasper was from the Texas cavalry, which designated the kind of costume he wore. They wore a yellow sash, but I used a red sash—it was prettier," she added with a laugh. "I loved the look of the scarlet with him riding on his horse."

Leah Gibson as Nettie, Catalina Sandino Moreno as Maria, and Kirsten Prout as Lucy.

Costume sketches for Maria and her cohorts.

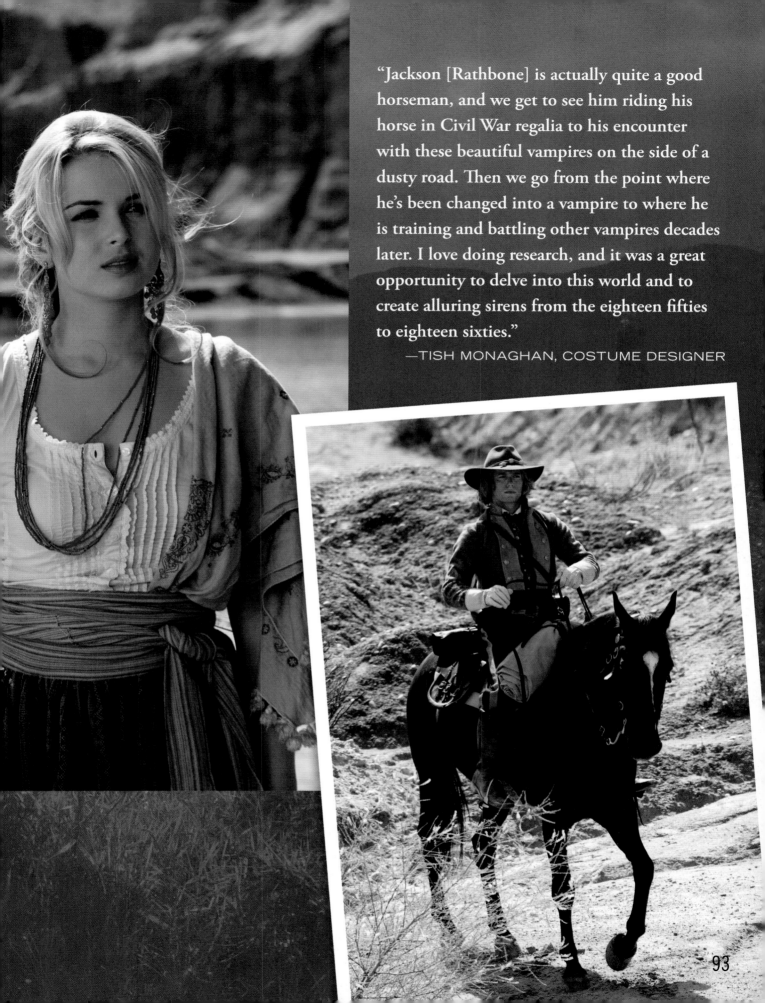

"Jackson [Rathbone] is actually quite a good horseman, and we get to see him riding his horse in Civil War regalia to his encounter with these beautiful vampires on the side of a dusty road. Then we go from the point where he's been changed into a vampire to where he is training and battling other vampires decades later. I love doing research, and it was a great opportunity to delve into this world and to create alluring sirens from the eighteen fifties to eighteen sixties."

—TISH MONAGHAN, COSTUME DESIGNER

Moreno as Maria.

The newborn soldiers
Jasper will train.

Monaghan continued. "When we first see Jasper, he's dirty and broken down. So we had to paint and sand the uniform to create the variations and hues that would make it look worn from six months of traveling the dusty trails of Texas. When we see him decades later, when he's training vampires, his uniform is in disrepair. He's just wearing his vest and shirt, which are stained and aged. We took his jacket and sash and put them on the character of Maria, the one who turned him into a vampire . . . and is more or less controlling him. That was my idea, and I thought it worked well. It was an easy way to indicate she was . . . in control."

Maria's army of newborns would represent a cross section of victims and reinforce the notion, as seen with Victoria and the other nomadic vampires of *Twilight*, that vampires can become scavengers who might wear the clothing of their victims. "For the various newborn soldiers Jasper would either be training or battling, I gave them some remnants of Civil War uniforms and clothing they could have stolen from their victims, from whatever walk of life," Monaghan added.

The scene of the Texas cavalryman riding through the dust and encountering the vampire sirens blended two locations that were hours apart. The opening images required the second unit to journey into the interior of British Columbia to film actor Jackson Rathbone against the flat vistas the director wanted. "It was about three, four hours outside Vancouver," second-unit makeup lead JoAnn Fowler recalled. "There was this beautiful land of sagebrush and cactus, with heat over a hundred degrees, almost like a desert in the interior."

That interior region had been an easy choice for the wide shots that would be picked up by the first unit, as it was a known venue for filmmakers wanting to shoot a Western or anything requiring desert country. But it was decided that the first-unit work of Jasper's meeting with Maria and the other vampire sirens had to be shot in the Vancouver area. But how were they going to find a little piece of Texas desert in the city? Production designer Paul Austerberry had an idea.

"Years ago I did a BMW commercial, and I used a rock quarry in Ontario to have these

Roman soldiers and Roman chariots riding through," Austerberry recalled. "I mentioned that I had been able to find a rock quarry, which was a location similar to what we needed for the Texas desert, so why don't we see if there was a quarry around Vancouver we could use? We found one, although it was actually more of a gravel pit than a rock quarry. It had soft, sandy embankments, which better matched the desert feel we shot for the wider stuff. They had a big pump at this site, but it kept filling up with water. What was amazing, and what I didn't expect, was it had this big body of water that gave us bright, beautiful reflections in the moonlight and had these beautiful, naturally eroded cliffs."

The erosion emulated what Bill Bannerman noted was a hoodoo effect, the process of wind and weathering that produces spires of rock, or hoodoos. For the sequence in which the young Confederate soldier meets the vampire women, the landscape gave an authentic touch. "This quarry on the outskirts of Vancouver looked rustic and weathered in a badlands or northern Texas Panhandle way," Bannerman said. "This open pit had been mined out and turned into sand. It had deteriorated over time; the constant rains . . . weathered it away and gave the kind of hoodoo effect indigenous to the western Rockies and Canada. Certain parts of the sediment had the shapes of mushrooms sitting on little sand pyramids. It gave a Western feel."

The scene at the quarry where Jasper met Maria marked the first day of principal photography. During the preceding weekend, fifty-foot Technocranes for cameras were brought in—and began to sink into the ground. "What we thought was solid sand was actually quite mushy underneath," Austerberry recalled. "It became a bit like quicksand. So we had to bring in tons of gravel just for an access road for this camera position, to get the Technocrane in the right spot to film the horse. The horse had to plod through some of the water, and our horse wrangler said it was too mushy. So we had to bring in gravel and fill it in and let the water pump up just enough to cover the gravel to make it sturdy underneath for the horse. I had known we'd have to get more gravel for the horse, but we didn't expect to have to do gravel work for the equipment. When the grips brought in that big crane and it began to sink—it was a bit of a panic for a while."

The crisis passed, the location was made ready that weekend, and shooting began as scheduled on Monday. "For the quarry, we had our greens department bring in sagebrush and dried greens to match [the desert location]," Austerberry added. "They shot day for night, meaning it was filmed in daylight and would be exposed much darker to look like nighttime— the same technique as the old spaghetti westerns where Clint Eastwood used to ride across the desert. Those scenes that we shot at the quarry were quite wonderful."

The Vancouver quarry that filled in as a Texas location.

An Interview with Nikki Reed ❦ Rosalie Hale ❦

"[The first movie] developed into something bigger than any of us anticipated, and it is amazing because we are all going through it together. All of us cast members have gotten along from the very beginning. It's really important to create a trusting bond with your cast, especially when you will be a part of each other's lives for so long.

"When you are playing someone who looks so drastically different from yourself, you never really feel like the character until after hair and makeup is done. It takes hours to look like Rosalie, so I usually have a nap in the makeup chair. I go to sleep Nikki and wake up Rosalie.

"I am very maternal, like Rosalie. I am also very tough, and I'm not afraid to say what is on my mind. Sometimes I wish I could filter my thoughts, but at least I don't leave people guessing.

"I've become less and less afraid to experiment, and I've learned how to be consistent with my character, as well as allowing her to grow with each film. . . . We had a lot of fun shooting the third film, because there was more for us to do and tons of action!

Rosalie and Emmett.

"I have really loved the process of working with each director. I think all three have been incredible, but very different. They all brought something new to the table, and it's been interesting to really commit to each director's vision and understand their perspective. I have learned so much about myself as an actor, and as a person, from this process.

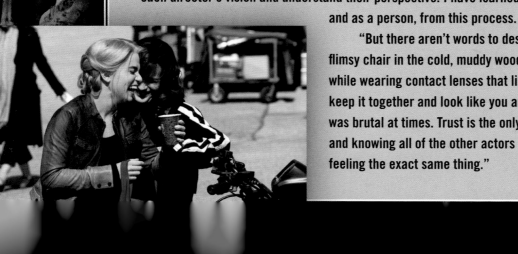

"But there aren't words to describe what it feels like to sit on a flimsy chair in the cold, muddy woods with rain pouring down on you while wearing contact lenses that limit your vision, all the while trying to keep it together and look like you are hunting down another vampire. It was brutal at times. Trust is the only thing that gets you through it. That, and knowing all of the other actors and crew members are thinking and feeling the exact same thing."

An Interview with Jackson Rathbone ❧ Jasper Hale ❧

"Both sequels to *Twilight* have felt like a family reunion. The series has been a growing experience for all of us, and we've grown together like a family.

"I would define acting as 'Wear what you want to wear, say what you want to say, and never lie.' I think it's important to do research when bringing a literary character to life. I've read the books along with each script to get a sense of the overall story. I try to put all of myself into everything I do, whether or not it's anything like my normal life. I try to learn from all my past endeavors, and I love getting to fully flesh out a character. With a series like *The Twilight Saga*, I've gotten to develop Jasper over the course of three movies and, therefore, it gets easier to play it honestly, which is what it's all about.

"In the morning [during hair, makeup, and costume] you literally watch yourself become the image of the character, and your body posture and overall feelings change accordingly. By the time you get on set, you're fully in your character's skin.

"I would definitely say the most intense scenes in the series are the action scenes in *Eclipse*. The Cullens have to face off against a vampire army, so there were a lot of fight scenes where we each had to fight multiple opponents. That did get intense but, I think, was also the most fun. *Eclipse* is an action-packed romantic film, with a dark undertone to this life that Bella is fully realizing as it unfolds around her in the form of werewolves and the vampire army—that's a whole new reality for a girl who is still in high school.

"I've been asked whether [the success of *New Moon* changed my life] and I can honestly say my life is still the same. I'm still acting and making music and other forms of art—that will never change. I'm just blessed to have a larger audience to play to now. As a performer, that's a dream come true."

Alice and Jasper share a kiss.

Jack Huston as Royce King II and Nikki Reed as Rosalie Hale.

In the ECLIPSE novel, Rosalie finally reaches out to Bella with something she wants to share.

"Would you like to hear my story, Bella? It doesn't have a happy ending—but which of ours does? If we had happy endings, we'd all be under gravestones now. . . . I lived in a different world than you do, Bella. My human world was a much simpler place. It was nineteen thirty-three. I was eighteen, and I was beautiful. My life was perfect."[5]

Rosalie was betrothed to Royce King, a young man she thought loved her as much as she loved him, and she had dreams of raising a family. Her dreams died on the cold pavement of a city street where she was beaten and left for dead.

> "BELLA WANTS TO BE A VAMPIRE, AND ROSALIE REPRESENTS THE CONSEQUENCES OF THAT CHOICE."

Once again, Carlisle Cullen would discover a young person whose life was ebbing away and choose to save it by changing her. For Rosalie, it was the end of mortal dreams and the beginning of eternal regret.

"Rosalie's is a grim story," screenwriter Rosenberg observed. "It was a challenge and took many drafts getting into it, and I'm sure David Slade did many drafts in the editing room. Her story was, thematically, connected to the whole theme of the movie, which is choice and the consequences of choice. Bella wants to be a vampire, and Rosalie represents the consequences of that choice. As a vampire, Rosalie can't have children, and it's driving that home for Bella. Jacob represents

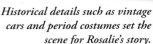

Historical details such as vintage cars and period costumes set the scene for Rosalie's story.

a choice where you can have children and a normal life. Bella has a choice—Rosalie had no choice."

Rosenberg emphasized Rosalie's story by positioning it in a new place in the story line. "The Rosalie scene was born out of the scene prior to it, which was a nonphysical confrontation between Edward and Jacob. Right before that, Bella had punched Jacob because he had made his intentions known but had been wildly inappropriate. Edward and Jacob represent two sides of a choice, and Bella's anger at Jacob has an element of anger at herself for denying the option of her own feelings for Jacob."

When principal photography began, the production had not yet locked into an exterior location for what Rosenberg noted in the script was Rochester, New York. Vancouver wasn't the best city for 1930s period architecture, although there were "very small pockets," Paul Austerberry noted. "The flashback stories were important because they're quite poignant and character-building points for the vampire characters, the first time we get to know their history. It was very important to nail down that period and the feel of that period. We scoured the city, and

it turned out the right location was right under our noses."

Downtown, right by the Hotel Vancouver, was the Vancouver Art Gallery, housed in a turn-of-the-century building. The production design team felt they just needed to look in two directions to get a slice of the time period. "The front of the Art Gallery had modern sculptures and fountains," said Austerberry, "but we used the side of the building [that] had, diagonally opposite, the Hotel Vancouver, which was mostly intact, periodwise. Luckily, leaves were still on the trees and blocked a lot of modern stuff."

Bill Bannerman and David Slade scouted the location and loved it. Bannerman was then back at his chessboard plotting the next move. "I sat down with my team—the location manager, assistant director, and the various captains of each department—and we went over the red-flag list and to-do list," Bannerman explained. "We needed to control the filming at night, we needed to abate any signage from the nineteen forties onward, [and] we had to bring in period cars. The team then went off to execute those details. A little bit of tweaking from the art department, positioning the camera to frame out the contemporary architecture, and peppering the street with nineteen-thirties vehicles completely sold the period."

The production design team and the art department also added period lighting fixtures that Javier Aguirresarobe could use as practical foreground lighting elements. For the night scene, any neon and telltale traffic lights were blocked out with a ten-foot-high period newspaper stand that was built.

Meanwhile, the costume designer headed to Los Angeles to rent the period clothes necessary for Rosalie and her fiancé, along with a wardrobe sufficient to dress forty to fifty extras for the daytime scenes. "The [decade] was about very sensual, beautiful fabrics," Monaghan said.

Rosalie's betrothed, Royce, and his male friends were turned out in 1930s style with three-piece suits and fedoras. When actor Jack Huston came to the set in the morning to film the scene of Royce strolling with his fiancée, hair department lead Sherritt got a surprise—the actor had shoulder-length hair, not the close-cropped look of a wealthy young man of the time. "This was the first time Tish [Monaghan] and I had met him, and he's supposed to go before

Costume sketch for Rosalie Hale's 1930s ensemble.

camera that day with a Clark Gable look, not hair down to his shoulders!" Sherritt said, laughing. "This kind of situation actually comes up a lot. He had his hair long for another role, and we couldn't cut it. But it was up to us to create the character the production wants. He wore a hat in the scene, so Stacey, my right-hand gal, and I put his hair up and under his fedora."

For Rosalie's last night of humanity, she was dressed in a skirt and a blouse, a camel wrap coat, and a beret. That fateful night she discovers Royce and his friends cavorting in the street, and she is unhappy at their boorish behavior. "She's walking home and en route she encounters her fiancé, and he's drunk and standing on the street with three friends," Monaghan said. "She says something about his behavior that upsets him, he takes affront, and they beat her. They leave her for dead. Carlisle finds her and he turns her." As a vampire, Rosalie exacts her terrible revenge, swooping in and killing her murderers.

"Rosalie's story is one that surprises us, and the photography was meant to follow this path," observed Javier Aguirresarobe. "We go from bright scenes where we see this girl's naive happiness to the sordidness of dark streets full of bad omens. In warm tones, we move between light and shadows."

> "ROSALIE'S STORY IS ONE THAT SURPRISES US, AND THE PHOTOGRAPHY WAS MEANT TO FOLLOW THIS PATH."

Rosalie (Reed) meets her end as a human.

"In light of Jasper's and Rosalie's backstories, Bella is forced to reexamine her decision to become a vampire. When Jasper recounts the bloodlust of being a newborn and his harsh life as a warrior, Bella realizes that she's entering a life of violence and danger, which may complicate the happiness she seeks with Edward. Rosalie laments the fact that she can never have a child, which is another thing that Bella hadn't thought of. Is she willing to give up being a mother herself? Each of these backstories helps Bella realize that she's facing a choice that has real consequences."

—WYCK GODFREY, PRODUCER

A Newborn Threat

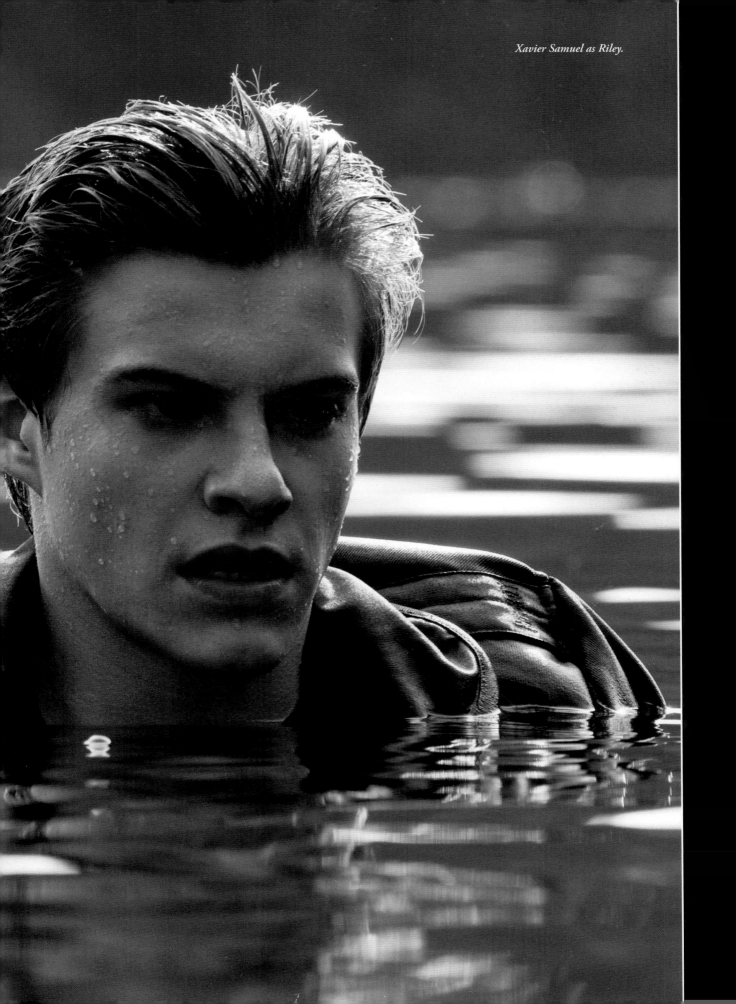

Unlike the other films, with their emphasis on gothic romance, the third film was darker, more threatening and violent. "As Bella gets closer and closer to becoming a vampire, there is danger and all these forces descending upon Forks," Wyck Godfrey observed. "Victoria and the newborns are coming from Seattle, the Volturi are coming—it all creates a heightened danger in the midst of Bella and Edward's decision to marry."

The battle against Victoria and her army required massive location and set work. It was a sequence divided between the big battle as the Cullens and the wolves fight the newborns and a final fight to the death between Victoria, Riley, and Edward.

"The bare elements of a fight component require a division between stunt players and real actors: What can the real actors do? How far do you go to the threshold of their physical capabilities before you hand off to a stunt person?" noted co-producer Bill Bannerman. "Well, that defines a training program. For the hero Cullen family actors, they arrived in Vancouver prior to shooting and hit the ground running with training, a basic health regimen, and getting into fight choreography and the basic moves of fight training. We scheduled the battle sequence for the latter part of the shooting schedule, which enabled them to take advantage of downtime to practice with our stunt coordinator and fight choreographer. [This way] when filming began, the actors were ready to hit their beats without compromise while making whatever modifications were needed to adjust for the lights and cameras."

Second-unit director E. J. Foerster blocks out a scene on set with Reed and Rathbone.

"Real fighting is tight and efficient, but in the movies you have to have 'line recognition.' The audience has to be able to see the moves. It's a new language of movement. The fighting style for a movie depends on the characters and the individual actors. For the vampires of *Eclipse*, it was about accentuating their speed. Vampires try to get around an opponent as fast as they can, and when they see an opening, they go in and finish it. If the neck or a limb is exposed, they'll try to rip it off. We kept the basic fighting style from *New Moon*, so you don't see them throwing kicks and punches. For David [Slade] it was about big impacts and big hits, keeping it mean and efficient."

—JONATHAN EUSEBIO, FIGHT COORDINATOR

Carlisle (Facinelli) and Edward (Pattinson) have fun mock-fighting each other.

For the fight training, the production team brought in Jonathan Eusebio, who had recently worked on *Iron Man 2*. "Jonathan lives in a world where if you fail to plan, you plan to fail," Bannerman added. "He gets one hundred percent success because he does the homework and rehearsals required to pull things off on the required day. Jonathan is an advocate of rehearsal time so the actors will be able to do it in their sleep."

Eusebio specializes in fight choreography and training for movies. A competitive kickboxer in the early 1990s, Eusebio had three trainers who became stuntmen—Chad Stahelski doubled for Keanu Reeves in the *Matrix* movies, and David Leitch and Damon Caro doubled for Brad Pitt and Ed Norton, respectively, in *Fight Club*—and he followed them into the business. An early break for Eusebio was training actor Matt Damon for *The Bourne Identity*.

Eusebio, Jon Valera, and Jackson Spidell came to Vancouver to design the fight choreography and literally get the actors into fighting shape on an extremely tight schedule. "Being in shape and in fighting shape are equally impor-

tant," Eusebio noted. "But you have to look the part. All the nuances and body mechanics have to be there."

Training began with an assessment of each actor's physical abilities, including stretching to ascertain flexibility, going through basic "movie style" punches, kicks, and stances, and moving on to drills that broke off bits of fight choreography to see how quickly the actor could pick up the moves. Although Eusebio explained that conditioning and fight training usually happen on the same day, the regimen was broken up into fight training on Monday, Wednesday, and Friday, with weight and fitness training on alternate weekdays. "We choreographed a 'skeleton' of the fight and drilled them on that, and everything progressed from there," Eusebio recalled. "The longer you train, the better, so your body will remember the movements. It takes, like, a thousand reps before it starts feeling like a natural motion."

The training also took into account the ability of vampires to jump at great heights through the air. That meant stunt coordinator Stoneham's wirework, where the apex of the arc of a vampire's leap might be fifteen to twenty feet off the ground.

An Interview with Peter Facinelli ❧ Dr. Carlisle Cullen ❧

"I read *Twilight* the day before I met Catherine [Hardwicke], to prep for my meeting with the director, and fell in love with it. I understand what it's like being the patriarch of a family, having kids myself. I also like to think that I share Carlisle's compassion and a love for humanity.

"Having different directors keeps the material fresh. They bring their own vision to each film, and each director continues to push us to look at our characters in new ways. The most intense scene for me, and also the most fun, was the battle sequence in *Eclipse*. We worked on fight training for about six weeks, and when we finally got to put it all into action, it was intense.

"To me, acting is an art, one that is difficult to explain. If I attempted to break it down, I would define it as interpreting a set of given circumstances and fully committing yourself in those circumstances while reacting truthfully as the character you are portraying.

"Sometimes, people will ask me to say a line from the movies and I have to decline. Without the costume, hair, and makeup, it just doesn't work. The process of being transformed after I put on the clothes, style the hair, put in the [contact lenses], and have the makeup on—it's a ritual that helps me to get into that character. When I look into a mirror and see Carlisle, I am taken into that world."

An Interview with Elizabeth Reaser ❧ Esme Cullen ❧

"Before I got cast I hadn't read the books. But as soon as I was cast, I bought the books and didn't leave the house for a week.

"Most movies are finite, most characters you put to bed when you wrap. But the experience of playing a character in a series is unique, with *Twilight* you get to stay with a character. This is interesting to me, because I'm endlessly curious about Esme. Working with a different director for each film has been exciting to see how each thinks, how they shoot. Each one has inspired me to think about Esme in a different way.

"I think our cast has become some version of a family. We've done three movies together, we've holed up together, been on location for months at a time. And I think Peter [Facinelli] really is the head of 'our family.' He's just that guy.

"Hair and makeup is an intense process when you're playing a Cullen. It informs how you feel and move. But it can be a challenge at times because it's inhibiting—you have to be careful not to mess it up! Shooting in the freezing rain in the middle of a forest with vampire hair and makeup has been a challenge from the very beginning. But the locations are hauntingly beautiful and really evoke the world of the books.

"Surprisingly, the most fun for me was all the action stuff in *Eclipse*. Those scenes were scary to shoot, physically scary. I'd never done anything like that."

Alice (Greene) kicks some newborn vampire butt.

"THE MAIN BATTLE IS COMPLETE MAYHEM."

newborn is attacking a Cullen, another newborn will just go over him. They're like wild animals."

The fighting style Eusebio's team developed for the Cullens was based on the personality of each character. Rosalie was a bit of a "dirty fighter," Eusebio noted. Emmett was the strongest, and his prowess included big throws and physical action. Alice the telepath was sleek and agile. Edward had superspeed.

The fight choreography had to take into account all the complex bits and pieces of the five Cullen characters and some twenty newborn stunt performers, special effects and the stunt coordinator's wirework, and the computer-generated wolves that would be added in postproduction. Nothing was "linear," the fight coordinator commented. Although such complicated scenes are often developed completely in digital animatics, with CG figures and environments, because of the tight schedule *The Twilight Saga: Eclipse* director relied on traditional drawn storyboards to design the action.

"Working on the battlefield location, which was a clearing at the foot of the mountains, was definitely different than working on a stage environment," Bill Bannerman said. "Wires and pulleys and computerized descenders work beautifully in an air-controlled, zero-humidity environment. But it rains seventy percent of the year in the foothills of North Vancouver, so you have to be able to adapt to external conditions and achieve the same kind of efficiency. You can't lose orientation, because everything is now extremely external."

Since the actors would be strapped into a harness and fighting gravity as they were suspended and flown, they had to train in the rigs long enough to make it appear natural and effortless when they performed one of those astounding leaps for the camera. The production needed something more than a conventional gym, and the team found a small Vancouver soundstage where the existing ceiling grid allowed them to set up the wire system.

"The main battle is complete mayhem," fight coordinator Jonathan Eusebio said. "The Cullens are more controlled, while everything with the newborns is wild and frenetic. We designed the newborns almost like army ants. They swarm, with no regard for each other. If a

The battleground was a brand-new location, Bannerman revealed, one in an orbit that included some iconic *Twilight Saga* locations. "[There] was our beautiful meadow with all the flowers, and another quarter mile down the road was where we found the clearing that would accommodate the final conflict. It was a beautiful location, with mountainous backgrounds. It was actually a gun range. . . . The targets [were cleared out], and we came in with all our paraphernalia. We put down soft pads, used cranes to pre-rig a vampire rig-and-truss system for the wirework and all the lighting [equipment]. The complexity of the shoot required four weeks of shooting between the first and second units."

"The battle was staged piece by piece," stunt coordinator John Stoneham Jr. noted. "It rained a lot, but then we'd have sunshine when we needed overcast because vampires sparkle

IT BECAME A BATTLE AGAINST THE ELEMENTS.

in the sun. So the grips for the DP set up a big tarp that was maybe twenty by sixty feet and could be moved around to block out the sun. Our wire rigs were twenty to forty feet off the ground, and this tarp was above us, at fifty or sixty feet in the air."

"In Vancouver, you do not get consistent weather during a four-week period," Bannerman added, "so our setup included a pre-rigged truss system where we hung silks, like the ceiling of a circus tent, to control lighting conditions for Javier. We wanted things to be comfortable for our DP."

It became a battle against the elements, with Eusebio and his crew playing the roles of coaches and motivators for the actors who had to perform in what were often rainy and cold conditions. "Vampires aren't supposed to feel heat and cold, so they had to maintain that appearance in those wet and cold conditions," Eusebio explained.

The final shot will show computer-generated wolves watching the vampires practice fighting techniques. On set, wolf cutouts stood in.

"The training scenes and the final battle take place in different forests. What unites the two places is a feeling of anxiety and fear. There is no sun, and the light is stuck in a downtime. It is a gray and expectant atmosphere. In the battle sequences, visual effects are used to show the fighting abilities of the werewolves and the Cullens as they join together against the cruelty of the newborn invaders. *Eclipse* is a film that alternates powerful and violent action with an intensity not seen in the other films in the series."

—JAVIER AGUIRRESAROBE, DIRECTOR OF PHOTOGRAPHY

"What I love about *Eclipse* is we join forces with the wolves. I personally love the wolves. They smell gross [to vampires], there's the whole treaty, we don't like them. But Esme doesn't hate them. It's fun that we join forces, that we teach each other, that we connect."

—ELIZABETH REASER, ACTRESS

Ashley Greene as Alice Cullen, Nikki Reed as Rosalie Hale, Elizabeth Reaser as Esme Cullen, Jackson Rathbone as Jasper Hale, and Peter Facinelli as Carlisle Cullen.

"When we see Riley heading the army, he's like a hipster general, with a three-quarter-length jacket, a button-up shirt, and skinny burgundy jeans. For the battle itself, the Cullens are dressed in black or very dark clothing—a 'stealth machine' is how I envisioned them as a group. I wanted the audience to see who was who, since there was a lot of stunt action and the battle is set in misty elements. There are also scenes of them running through the forest, and I wanted to silhouette them nicely against the trees. So there is a progression from the lighter colors of their outfits in the initial chase of Victoria, their training, and the darker colors of the final battle."

—TISH MONAGHAN, COSTUME DESIGNER

There would be no CG newborns, and since the rabid vampires would be wrestling with, jumping on, strangling, throwing, and generally mixing it up with the ferocious wolves, the stunt performers needed something physical to interact with. Alex Burdett's special effects department built six-to-eight-foot-long beanbags to Tippett Studio's specifications. Each one was called a "potato," and it simulated the scale of a werewolf's torso during physical stunts. (Image Engine used a similar object when creating its ancient wolves for the Quileute story.) Four potatoes made of foam and covered with tracking marks enabled Tippett Studio to line up and replace the proxy object with their character animation. Despite its bulky size, each potato weighed only twenty pounds, which made it easier to rig and throw into the action.

"The battle sequence was pretty well storyboarded, and Phil [Tippett] and I had pretty tight discussions with the stunt coordinators about the rigs that would be built for the potato," explained visual effects supervisor Eric Leven. "Sometimes it was as simple as having a couple stunt guys

"I've looked forward to *Eclipse* because my character has been getting larger and larger, and *Eclipse* has a lot of fighting and stunt scenes, which I love to do. We had a great stunt crew that taught us a bunch of fighting techniques. I've been boxing for a long time, [and] I've done some jujitsu, so it was fun challenging myself with some of the stuntmen who have done amazing movies. Emmett, you know, he loves to fight. He's just a bulldozer—he goes through and takes care of business."

—KELLAN LUTZ, ACTOR

The "potato" stood in for
CG wolves during stunt shots.

"I've gotten better at writing action. You get to choreograph movement on the page, and you try to find ways to describe that. The fun is in the story-telling. For example, in the first act, during the early chase after Victoria, Paul and Emmett went at it. They had a physical confrontation, so the animosity between them was a little story point. So for the final battle, I wrote that Paul and Emmett team up; you see that they're working together. That little story of Paul and Emmett and their rapprochement puts the button at the end of that narrative thread."

—MELISSA ROSENBERG, SCREENWRITER

standing off-camera and literally throwing it at a newborn stunt performer and having that performer grab it and fall to the ground as if he had been tackled by a werewolf. Other times, the potato was on a rig five feet off the ground, which is the height of a wolf, and suspended so an actor could jump on top of it."

To replace the potato with the CG were-wolves required a lot of extra digital work, Leven noted. "Our beanbag was basically a static tube; it didn't have the reality of a thousand-pound werewolf thrashing around. What we found when we started putting in our CG wolves was they no longer covered up the beanbag. So we had to put in CG hands and arms [for the newborns] where necessary, and if a newborn was hanging off the wolf, we had to digit-ally paint the newborns back in. It was a balance of keeping as much of the practical actors from the location as possible while getting the performance animation we needed from the werewolves."

"WHEN SOMEONE BECOMES A VAMPIRE, THEIR MUSCLE FIBERS TURN INTO SOMETHING LIKE THE FACETS OF A CRYSTAL."

The Twilight Saga: Eclipse fully explores what Shawn Walsh, visual effects executive producer at Image Engine, calls "the shattering effect."

There had been a hint of the shattering-effect idea in New Moon during the fight in Volturi Hall, when Edward gets thrown on the marble floor and his face starts to crack but instantly heals. To achieve the effect, and to follow the production's marching orders of realism, Image Engine developed an entire vampire physiology. "The notion was that when a human is transformed into a vampire, they become these beautiful, pale creatures—but they can now punch a chunk out of a tree or smash through something," noted Image Engine visual effects supervi-sor Jon Cowley. "Since their skin glitters like a diamond in the sun, there was the idea that they have this hard, diamond-like quality. In the big battle, if a vampire is punched in the head it will

"We went by the notion that when a human is changed into a vampire, all of their anatomy—bone, fat, muscles, skin—become chemically changed. Vampire bones become harder and stronger than human bones, [and] muscles take on a different physical property. It all becomes more crystalline and diamond-like. To wrap our head around the concept, we had to think through the whole process, to understand all the stages."

—JON COWLEY, VISUAL EFFECTS SUPERVISOR, IMAGE ENGINE

Filming the Volturi approach after the battle.

shatter, so we needed to establish the look of what happens inside the body, how the pieces break."

"What are vampires made of? The answer had to be explicit, given the amount of vampire carnage audiences are likely to see," explained Jeremy Ball, visual effects coordinator. "For the most part, the 'vampire shattering' gags were accomplished with CG enhancements to practical stunts."

The effects artists showed the director real crystals as reference, trying to base the effect on scientific principles. "We wanted to underline that it's not magic, that there's a potential science behind all of this, that [their anatomy] turns into a different sort of property," Cowley added. "So, when someone becomes a vampire, their muscle fibers turn into something like the facets of a crystal, their skin becomes this hard exterior surface, but they can still move around, much like the chain mail a medieval knight would wear. A lot of that real-world property drove our design, [the idea] that if we start from that place it would be easy to create something that would look photo-realistic and that audiences could believe in."

"IN THE BIG BATTLE, IF A VAMPIRE IS PUNCHED IN THE HEAD IT WILL SHATTER."

Edward watches his enemies burn.

115

The Mount Seymour set for the campsite.

While the main battle rages, the final showdown takes place on a distant mountaintop. To keep the newborns off their trail, Jacob has used his wolf scent to disguise Bella as he takes her to the isolated mountaintop to meet Edward and spend the eve of battle in a tent. It would be a cold night, and in the morning they would discover that a storm had passed over and left a layer of snow. But despite their precautions, Victoria and Riley find them. "The battle in the book was over and done really quickly," the director observed. "In the film, the battle was all about the vampires and wolves working together, but the climax was always going to be the fight on the mountaintop, when Edward and Victoria have their battle to the death."

To realize that fight, the production team divided the sequence into two parts. The arrival at the mountaintop was staged on location on Mount Seymour, north of Vancouver. But there was no snow and, for ecological reasons, the production couldn't contaminate the wilderness with fake snow. They would have to bring the mountaintop to a soundstage.

"The mountaintop was a jigsaw of all these different puzzle pieces to figure out," Bill Bannerman explained. "The first part of the sequence we shot at a park adjacent to a ski hill with endless vistas that gave us an impressive production value. But when you're at an altitude of six thousand or seven thousand feet, the weather can be volatile; you can't predict it. So we needed to shoot quickly at that location. We downsized our basic needs for that location to one day of shooting. We got up there very fast in the morning and shot all day. Lucky for us, we had beautiful conditions and we were able to get safely off the hill by sunset. We shot everything to before the snowstorm, so when Bella comes out of the tent in the morning, there is snow everywhere—from that moment on, everything on the mountaintop is stage."

Paul Austerberry's production design and art department had plenty of location photos of the mountaintop, and the art department sent a survey team to the location. The story points also took the curse off having to perfectly replicate the physical location and specific landmarks. "The fact that they walk away from the tent and there's a passage of time saved us from having to be exact," Austerberry explained. "They arrive at the mountain, and you don't actually see them go into the tent. By the time they open up the tent, the storm has left a layer of snow, so things are magically different already. We weren't locked in one hundred percent to the mountain. We re-created the mountaintop

Lautner on location (above) and on the soundstage (right).

"It was amazing to go to Mount Seymour and see such beautiful, rugged wilderness within the zone of Vancouver. There was a ski hill, and we went beyond the chairlift. It had all the great vistas we needed for the approach as the characters arrive to set up camp, but we had to create snow, which we couldn't do at the park. But even if you shoot in real snow, you still have to use crushed-ice machines to blow [fresh layers of snow] and sweep out any tracks or footprints. So we re-created the wilderness in the studio and used paper products in that controlled environment."

—PAUL AUSTERBERRY, PRODUCTION DESIGNER

"We're on the tip-top of Mount Seymour, and it's gorgeous. That's where Bella and Jacob share their first real kiss."
—TAYLOR LAUTNER, ACTOR

with a cliff that didn't exist and trees that matched what we see on the mountain."

The soundstage set began with 3-D art department images and digital "previsualization" of the mountaintop that went to the construction department, which built a wooden framework that roughly corresponded to the 3-D outline. "We cast real foam rocks and created rock sheets that we screwed into this rough framework," Austerberry explained. "We patched and joined all the seams to give the rock face a uniform look. Then the bare rocks were painted. Some of the set was just foam—if you stepped in it, your foot would go through. A lot of what we needed to walk on was backed by plywood on the wooden stick frame. We had the greens team bring in real rocks, dirt, bushes, and big trees, which were brought in by cranes and which the grip department tied off to the ceiling of the stage."

The soundstage set was surrounded by greenscreen so visual effects could add in background images. The production designer was also specific that the big trees had to match the real location. "Trees that grow near sea level don't look the same as old trees at higher elevations, which take years to grow because of the harsher weather," Austerberry explained. "Our amazing greens team went three hours away to a logging preserve because I insisted we had to get the gnarled, bent, windblown trees we saw in daytime at the real location."

Alex Burdett and his special effects team then snowed in the set, spraying on finely chopped bits of paper that, when mixed with water, would stick to the set rock face and trees

"A set begins with discussions . . . then studying design plans and mock-ups in the art department, and visiting at least twice a week during the actual construction phase. We're involved in all the discussions and issues regarding the set. You intuitively know the set, every corner of it."

—ALEX BURDETT, SPECIAL EFFECTS SUPERVISOR

like the real thing. "I've been using this stuff for fifteen years," Burdett said. "It comes in bales that we'd churn up and mix with a little water and shoot through a hose. It's an art to apply, and we'd consult with the production designer and director on the look they wanted. Snow styles range from a heavy to frosty look, but for this they wanted it to look like the snow had fallen in one direction. We achieved a freshly fallen effect by spraying off of lifts, so it would gently and evenly fall across the set."

The special effects work included creating a forty-foot-tall tree of aluminum with foam bark, which actor Robert Pattinson could push over during the fight. "The tree was on a hinge with a safety," Burdett explained, "and on a cue we would release the safety and off the top we'd pull with an air ratchet, which gave it the momentum to bring it down over its fulcrum. How fast we pulled is how fast it fell."

The Twilight Saga: New Moon's Volturi Hall was arguably *the* set of the series, a classic space of faux marble that did justice to the power of the ancient vampires—but Bill Bannerman put the mountaintop set on a par with Volturi Hall. "Building that mountain inside a stage, we had to not only cater to the believability of the real location but all the

During the fight, Edward (Pattinson) pushes over a forty-foot-tall aluminum tree that Victoria (Howard) rides to the ground.

fight scene needs, with rigging for breakaway trees and wire rigging for the flying vampires, CG elements, the snow effect and mechanical effects component, greenscreen control, lighting needs. It was massive in its detail, coordination, and construction. The stage was twenty thousand square feet, and the set was fifteen thousand feet of that.

"The delicacy of that set construction was in vertical angles of rock faces and areas that were great to look at but [that] you could neither stand upon or touch. The set itself was fairly flat, with undulating areas and one little bowl area where the tent was. The rest was the rock faces that protruded upward and out of shot against the greenscreen. We had a ribbon around the edge that was probably fifteen feet deep all the way around to keep people off the set, to keep the virgin feel of a freshly snow-capped mountaintop."

Image Engine took care of the greenscreen work and digitally massaged the location footage, including a scene in which Jacob and Bella stand on a ridge for an intimate moment before night comes and the snow falls. "Our challenge was to make sure the location work and stage work matched, that they looked like they were in the same world," said sequence supervisor Robin Hackl. "They shot on Mount Seymour on a bright day with the sun beaming down, while they went for a more ambient overcast look when they filmed onstage. So we had to make it a little more overcast [in the location footage]. For the greenscreen set we added set extensions, sky replacement angles, and matte paintings that included distant mountains."

"As a fighter, Victoria is almost like Edward. She's really fast. She's normally very calculated and has been carefully plotting her revenge, but now that she finally faces her lover's killer, she becomes more ferocious. She lets loose."

—JONATHAN EUSEBIO, FIGHT COORDINATOR

121

At the moment when it appears Victoria has the upper hand, an unlikely person comes to the rescue—Bella herself. In the novel, Bella similarly wanted to assist her love, who is risking his life to save her, and she picks up a shard with the idea of drawing blood and distracting Victoria—but she doesn't actually do it. The screenwriter decided to take the scene further.

"In the third-wife story, the chief's wife stabs herself to keep the vampire from killing the head wolf," Rosenberg noted.

"It seemed to me that since Bella has taken in the story of the third wife, she should stab herself in her arm so she will bleed and distract Victoria and Riley enough that Edward gets the edge. . . . I wanted Bella to display strength, which is tough when you're a human in a battle with mythical creatures."

"I WANTED BELLA TO DISPLAY STRENGTH."

Jodelle Ferland as Bree Tanner.

Young actress Jodelle Ferland stepped into the role of Bree Tanner without realizing that she would become a key character thanks to the late announcement of a new Stephenie Meyer novella, THE SHORT SECOND LIFE OF BREE TANNER, which was published just before the film release.

The director and the screenwriter were among a lucky few to get a sneak peek at the text, from which they could glean inspiration for realizing the newborn vampires on-screen. Screenwriter Melissa Rosenberg noted that in ECLIPSE, the army of newborns just appears; readers don't see how the group was formed. "In the movie, we see how Victoria puts her army together and uses Riley," said Rosenberg. "The newborns don't know who created them and why they're together until the last minute, because Victoria wants that element of surprise and doesn't want Alice to 'see' that. And, of course, the Cullens don't know who Riley is. The short story Stephenie shared has Bree looking at Riley from a distance, trying to understand what is going on."

"The newborns are not zombies, and they're not monsters," explains director David Slade. "They are essentially people who have no control when they smell blood.

"Bree was the character who best illustrated it—she gets a burning in her throat at the smell of blood, and there's a lack of control," he continued. "Newborns have no inhibitions, and they're full of paranoia. And if you're amid a pack of newborns, you are not safe. You're not even safe in a clan, where the members might kill each other."

Of course, Bree survives the battle only to meet her end at the hands of the Volturi, striking a sharp contrast between the Italian enclave of vampires and the Cullens that sets up the final conflict in the novels.

The Return of the Volturi

The Volturi arrive after the battle and show no mercy to Bree, the newborn the Cullens have spared. "The Volturi are the vampire police," David Slade observed. "They're invincible, unstoppable, and they scare Bella. At the end of *Eclipse*, when they arrive, Bree is there to show that you can't have a happy ending for everybody. Jasper has described how during the [vampire] wars in the eighteen hundreds, the Volturi were the ones who would come in and sort it all out. They're destabilizing to any harmony the Cullens want to achieve.

"The Cullens are trying not to lose their humanity, but humanity is beneath the Volturi. The battle for the soul, the battle for what is good, does not concern them. The Volturi remind you that no one else is really in control of their destiny in this world."

"The Volturi's arrival on the battlefield is an imaginative marvel," Javier Aguirresarobe declared. "Their bodies glide through the forest in silence, almost as if flying at ground level. The atmosphere is gray and threatening. The Volturi's presence is feared by all. The black capes make the figures of these merciless creatures stand out amid the fog of an icy evening. It's a monochromatic image, austere and harsh, one that exudes fear."

Stunt coordinator John Stoneham Jr.'s crew made the four Volturi—Jane, Felix, Demetri, and Alec—"float" across the ground. "We built a truss to support an overhead line from end to end," he noted. "The actors were in harnesses with pick points at the hips, three or four feet off the ground, and we used computer-controlled winches."

Costume designer Monaghan gave the Volturi a new and dramatic look. "I really wanted to capture the same feeling I had for *New Moon* but give it a little twist and create a strong visual impact for when we see them floating out of the forest in a cool morning mist. David Slade also wanted to see a lot of movement of fabric for this sequence, so in this one there's a lot more fabric. I gave them a strong sculptural element, so as they emerged from the forest you got a good sense of these strong shapes."

Dakota Fanning as Jane.

Charlie Bewley as Demetri.

Costume sketch for Jane.

Daniel Cudmore as Felix.

The Volturi were rigged to "glide" over the ground.

Cameron Bright as Alec.

"In *New Moon*, Jacob hated Edward with a passion. But now, in *Eclipse*, he's forced to team up with Edward to protect Bella, which forces him to get to know Edward a little more. In the tent scene, Jacob and Edward have a heart-to-heart talk while Bella is supposedly asleep. Edward can read my thoughts, so I ask him to let me in to pick through his thoughts. And he does open up a little bit; he lets Jacob know that he's thinking Jacob might be a better choice for Bella than he is. That scene was my favorite in the book, and [I think] our version has lived up to it."

—TAYLOR LAUTNER, ACTOR

Eclipse

*Robert Pattinson as
Edward Cullen.*

The Twilight Saga: Eclipse transitioned to postproduction. By mid-January, David Slade had completed his director's cut. After weeks in the editing suite, the film was ready to show to Summit. "The reaction was really good," Slade said soon after the screening. "I'm ebullient, buoyant. It was a tough shoot. There was so much story and the challenge of getting all of the characters there and shining."

At the end of postproduction came the color process, not only timing the final prints for theatrical release but changing, adjusting, and tweaking the entire color range. Given the confined space and intensity of *Hard Candy*, color was a key element of that film, Slade noted. His colorist for *Hard Candy*, Jean-Clement Soret, whose credits included *City of Lost Children* and *Slumdog Millionaire*, worked with Slade on *Eclipse*.

"Color is an important emotional trigger, and Javier and I talked a lot in preproduction about the colors of each scene and what the final color would be," Slade explained. "Color is an emotional component. You might not notice it, but you'll feel it. It's not about whether something should be warm or cold, mauve or red. It all depends upon what is needed for the scene."

For Tippett Studio, the color choices the director would make had consequences for the CG wolves, and the Tippett team made sure they had a first pass at the director's DI. "It was important, because all the wolves were supersensitive to color," Eric Leven noted. "The Jacob wolf, in particular, had a pretty sensitive color bandwidth, as it were. If you put a red-colored Jacob wolf against a greenish-blue forest background, all of a sudden that wolf loses some of that red color—which is what makes him Jacob!"

Meanwhile, some of the recurring sets were taken apart and put in storage. Although all sets are temporary, sets that might be reused are designed to be taken apart and put back together for the next production. Such were the Bella house location set and the Cullen house soundstage set, which had removable walls and component parts.

"The fans have been so passionate about the integrity of the story being kept in place, as has Summit," Bill Bannerman said. "From the start, the studio felt that our obligation was to fulfill the original signature of the books and what was set forth in *Twilight* [the movie]. We couldn't have done that with three different Cullen houses, and that was never the thinking. We had an obligation to be true to the tiniest things, from the look of the artwork on the walls to the color of the clothes. I think audiences today have been educated by technically advanced filmmaking, where a lot of time and detail is afforded,

"COLOR IS AN EMOTIONAL COMPONENT. YOU MIGHT NOT NOTICE IT, BUT YOU'LL FEEL IT."

which is so different from the way it was prior to the *Star Wars* mega-budget tent-pole franchise projects. Now audiences expect it. If they're excited about a series of books, they expect to have the same experience in a visual medium as they had in the literary mode."

"The success of the films can be credited to many creative folks, not to mention the rich and engaging story that was created by Stephenie Meyer," said Rob Friedman. "All of that said, it is the passionate and dedicated fans that have made *Twilight* the phenomenon it is today. Without their support, we would not have the opportunity to make these films. We have not only great produc-

tions but also a community of people around the world who love the franchise."

On a Saturday morning in early 2010, David Slade was sipping his coffee and reflecting on *The Twilight Saga: Eclipse*. A movie production has been likened to a complex equation, and it's the director who has to keep it all in his or her head. "Making a film *is* a complex equation that involves everything from color swatches to great arcs of character narrative," Slade concluded. "It's the color of a wall and how much light hits it. It's how many hairs are going to be on a computer-generated wolf."

> "WE HAD AN OBLIGATION TO BE TRUE TO THE TINIEST THINGS."

Bella (Stewart) has a difficult conversation with Jacob (Lautner).

"This series is absolutely a phenomenon. I've been in the movie business for twenty-five years, and I've never seen anything like it! Maybe it's the Internet, which has created this ocean of adoring fans—there were fans we saw in Italy on *New Moon* that were recognized from Vancouver! It's hard to fathom, but there are many different factors. The books created a great tide of their own; there was the popularity of the films and the popularity of the actors. I also applaud our actors for being able to withstand it, because it's relentless for them."

—TISH MONAGHAN, COSTUME DESIGNER

But given all the intricacies, logistics, and technical demands, did the director have the time to stand back and appreciate the wonder of it all? For Slade, it was less about being awestruck and more about moments of epiphany.

"You're so deep into it, you know? Every day people look to you, as the director, to lead them through. Maybe it's an actor with a question about their character, or it's pouring rain in a scene where there's not supposed to be rain, and everybody is miserable. Sure, you can look at something like the Cullen house set or the mountaintop set and it's pretty cool, but then you're on to the next question—in fact, even while you're thinking about how cool something looks, you're being asked a question!

"Everyone has a need, and you have to know the answer. But for me, being a director is such a rewarding occupation, despite all the frustrations and struggles.

"The position of director was not something I aspired to until I found myself in it. The most important thing was to be able to take the pictures out of my head and put them on the screen. I knew the technical side and was slowly getting to that point where I could do that, but somehow it was never as I imagined it. I remember the first time it happened for me was an old music video—'Oh, my God! That's *exactly* how I see it!' It was quite scary, actually. Today, at this point in my career, the preparation side is finely honed, and I have to work at the speed of my own thoughts.

"Sometimes I have to watch the action from the monitor to make sure the blocking and camera is right. As the scene plays out, and you're looking at an actor's performance, you see all the work that went into creating a moment of cinema. And then, at that moment when the scene is great and you see an actor at the top of their game, it can be an epiphany. The hairs on your arms stand up, it's emotional, and you feel everything you should feel when you're doing something wonderful."

"I'm used to creating a family on a movie, then finishing up and having real closure," Wyck Godfrey noted. "I've always been nomadic, finishing one movie and then being off to another production, another country. The most interesting thing for me on these films is it's like summer camp, where we're all going to see each other next summer. I've enjoyed slipping back into the family that we created with

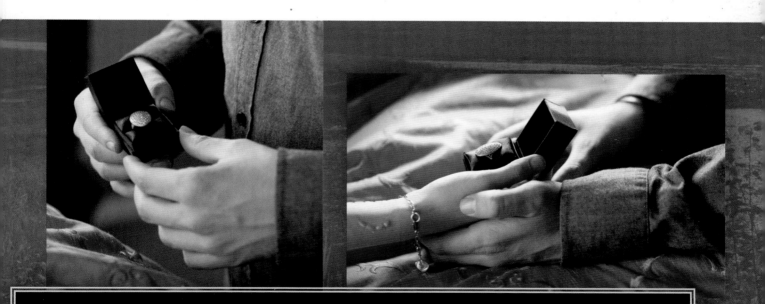

"Stephenie told me the idea she had when writing about the engagement ring was that Edward would give Bella the ring his mother had worn, a ring that would have been made in the late nineteenth century. . . . Stephenie explained it should extend from knuckle to knuckle. The stones should be tiny—like a pavé setting—with a slight curve to the surface. Ultimately, the ring that was built had over seventy tiny stones in it. It's truly unique."

—GILLIAN BOHRER, VICE PRESIDENT, PRODUCTION, SUMMIT

"It's always hard trying to improve a performance and make a gradual transition from the first two films, and with a new director who is bringing a whole load of different thoughts. My biggest hope is fans will see that all the films are connected and not just random installments. They are all set in a relatively short space of time, and there are subtleties in the relationships that have changed gradually. Hopefully, that kind of gradual development is visible to everyone."

—ROBERT PATTINSON, ACTOR

Twilight that has been carried on through *New Moon* and *Eclipse*. And now when I see Bella and Edward pop on the screen, a smile immediately comes to my face because I feel that I absolutely know them. In a normal film, you're being introduced to characters for the first time. I guess that's why people love movie franchises. They get to know characters throughout the series, and that makes them feel more participatory in the movie experience."

The audiences won't see what went on behind the scenes—the early-morning calls to the set, and the actors being transformed in the makeup trailers and by the hair and costume departments. They won't see the treks into the wilderness and mountaintops, the teeth-chattering bouts of rainy weather, the rehearsals and prep work and meetings. They won't see the cameras or the lights. Each puzzle piece has to be fit together into a seamless whole.

"One of the beauties of making a series of films is the continuity you can achieve with those working as cast and crew," said Wachsberger. "This extended family allows not only for consistent and efficient filmmaking, but also adds an extra layer of commitment to all who work on the productions, as they feel a part of something bigger."

David Slade directs Pattinson and Stewart.

But for all the hard work and long hours, there were those movie magic moments for the participants. "The magic is always there," said makeup artist JoAnn Fowler. "There's always some great scene being filmed, and you can watch talented actors pull it off. There's the magic of effects—we shot a snow-covered mountaintop in a studio, and they brought in real trees that smelled like Christmas. The stunts are stunning; a really good stunt is fantastic to watch. . . . You're always creating something really different; there's always the make-believe part. I'm always awed, no matter what movie I do."

"I am always pleasantly devastated by the talented actors in front of my lens, and honored by their trust in me. There's so much joy in making good stills. The whole cast and crew are all one big artist! Everyone's work goes into this giant effort that is filmmaking."

—KIMBERLEY FRENCH, SET PHOTOGRAPHER

"I think [the books] have such relatable emotions. Every one of us has been hurt by someone or something sometime in our lives. And the road to spiritual growth is the ability to forgive people who have hurt you.

"This whole experience has been sweet. When we did the first movie, Taylor was sixteen years old and quite a bit smaller than he is now. And to watch him grow up before my eyes—I'm just very proud of him. And the rest of the cast is like family. We're on our third movie now, and every time I come back on set it's like coming back home, you know."

—GIL BIRMINGHAM, ACTOR

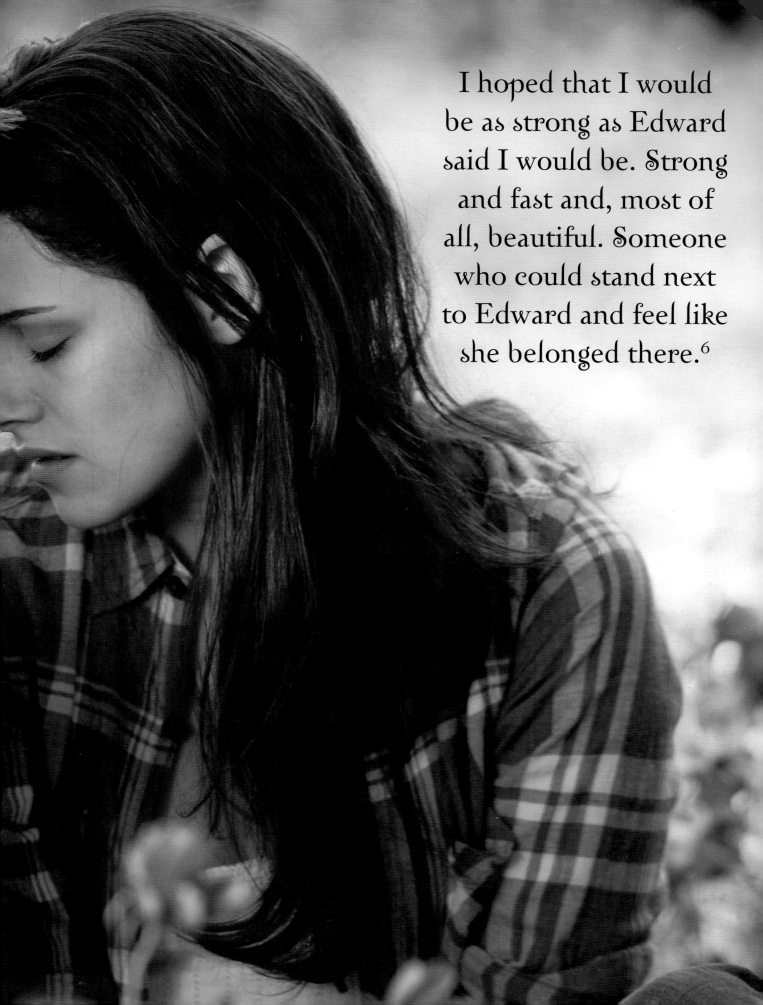

I hoped that I would be as strong as Edward said I would be. Strong and fast and, most of all, beautiful. Someone who could stand next to Edward and feel like she belonged there.[6]

NOTES

1:   Stephenie Meyer, *Eclipse* (New York: Megan Tingley Books, Little, Brown and Company, 2007), p. 379.

2:   Ibid., p. 263.

3:   Mark Cotta Vaz, *The Twilight Saga: New Moon: The Official Illustrated Movie Companion* (New York: Little, Brown and Company, 2009), p. 135.

4:   Meyer, *Eclipse*, pp. 240–241.

5:   Ibid., p. 154.

6:   Ibid., p. 344.

Except for interviews on pages 46, 47, 56, 57, 96, 97, 106, and 107, quotes from the actors are taken from the production's electronic press kits and are edited for continuity. The author thanks Summit Entertainment for making this material available for this book.

ACKNOWLEDGMENTS

My appreciation to Little, Brown and Company for entrusting me with documenting the making of the *Twilight* films, in particular editor Erin Stein, whose hard work and sublime eye made it all come together. My thanks as well to Summit Entertainment for facilitating access to the interview subjects, notably Eric Kops, who got things rolling, and Derek Schulte, who took it all the way. My special thanks to the many talented people who helped coordinate connections with those interview subjects: Erica Farjo in David Slade's office; Isaac Klausner in Wyck Godfrey's office; Gillian Smith at the ID agency for connecting me to Melissa Rosenberg; and Lori C. Petrini and Niketa Roman at Tippett Studio.

And here's a wolf-sized howl and shout-out to my agent, John Silbersack, for his time and amazing talent, and to his equally amazing assistant, Emma Beavers.

A tip of the old chapeau to the clan: my dad and Katherine, Maria, Patrick, Peter, and Teresa, as well as one of my favorite Twilighters, Katelin Vaz Labat, with a grand huzzah for Bettylu Sullivan Vaz, my mom and Exalted Reader of the Manuscripts. Visual effects wizard Bruce Walters worked his usual magic on the author's photo—thanks, Bruce! And best wishes to Jordan's Books for being so supportive over the years! And to Mike Wigner, world's greatest bicycle messenger—see you at Vesuvio's, Wig. It's a wrap.

Photo © Bruce Walters

AUTHOR'S CREDITS

Mark Cotta Vaz is the author of twenty-nine books. He wrote the companion books for *Twilight* and *The Twilight Saga: New Moon*, both of which were #1 *New York Times* bestsellers. His other works include the award-winning *The Invisible Art: The Legends of Movie Matte Painting* (co-authored with Oscar-winning filmmaker Craig Barron), the critically acclaimed biography *Living Dangerously: The Adventures of Merian C. Cooper, Creator of* King Kong, and *Industrial Light & Magic: Into the Digital Realm*, a chronicle of the second decade of the famed visual effects house.

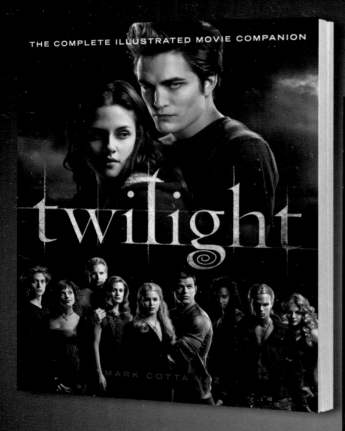

The #1 Bestselling Books That Started It All